SENATOR SAM ERVIN'S

Best Stories

Thad Stem, Jr.

and

Alan Butler

Moore Publishing Company
Durham, North Carolina

Library of Congress Catalog Card No. 73-86470
ISBN 0-87716-052-X   3 -28-74
                              9-25-74

This book is by two of North Carolina's outstanding writers and idea men. Moreover, it is timely not only for their state, but for the nation and the world.

It is about Sam Ervin, Jr.

That is the important fact. At this time in our nation's history it is important to know the human side of Senator Sam Ervin, and these stories reflect his humanity because they are part of him and are set in the North Carolina that he knows and loves. Always known as the Judge among his fellow senators, Sam Ervin was projected into the national spotlight by the Watergate hearings. He was not chosen by Majority Leader Mansfield at random. Sam Ervin has been the staunch defender of our United States Constitution since he joined that select club of 100. And the Watergate episode and its subsequent cover-up brought the Executive and Legislative branches to confrontation. Whether or not the shift of power to the Executive under strong presidents, and whether or not the Administration and/or Congress was spoiling for a fight are not issues of this book. Suffice it to say that many historical and current forces converged on the American nation and cast Senator Sam Ervin as an adversary of President Nixon.

Yet Sam Ervin is the reluctant inquisitor. Speaking kindly as a bible-quoting, country lawyer he admonishes and instructs, not only the overzealous wrongdoers but the rest of us as well. This is not the Harvard Law School part of his background but the small southern town Americana that we see. For a moment it is Uncle Sam giving all Americans a civics lesson, telling each of us that we can be better than we are, calling on us to defend our country by defending the virtues of democracy.

From their long and personal knowledge of the Judge and Senator, the authors focus on the man behind the institution. Long after the conflicts are past, the presidency will still be intact, the heavens will not have fallen, and our people can still read the best stories of a country lawyer who loves America.

Eugene V. Grace, M. D.
Publisher

Also by Thad Stem, Jr.

Picture Poems

The Jackknife Horse

The Animal Fair

The Perennial Almanac

Penny Whistles and Wild Plums

Light and Rest

Spur Line

A Flagstone Walk

P.T.A. Fifty Years Impact
Journey Proud
Entries From Oxford

Tar Heel Press

PREFACE

Since Senator Sam Ervin's ancestors were among the first to settle in the Morganton and Burke County area, his family is almost as old as civilization is old in the mountains of North Carolina. Indeed, the very sound of two family names, Ervin and Avery, conjure the enduring strength and grace of the Senator's beloved hills.

While Sam Ervin did not come into this world with a silver spoon in his mouth, he was born with an abiding reverence for four great traditions — Judeo-Christian ethics, Greek aesthetics, Roman law, and the hope and practical application of these three in democratic American society.

And along with this inherent reverence there is an innate affection for the bon mot, the mot juste, the ringing passage of heroic poetry, and all the fascinating stories of his fellow men and what it is that makes them laugh, cry, sweat, toil, sing, rejoice for the sweet-tasting delights of creation, and demonstrate that quiet type of courage which expresses itself as grace amid travail.

Few moderns have come into the world with such a vibrant sense of history. With Cicero, Senator Sam is aware that not to know what happened before one was born is to remain a child, always. He is aware every hour of his life that to be ignorant of the past is to be doomed to repeat the worst of yesterday's mistakes. Few men, by act and percept, have translated so fully and beautifully into their own lives the admonition of the late R.D.W. Connor: "Any society that is not interested in preserving its own history isn't likely to make any history that anyone else will want to read."

While it was Watergate that focused international attention on Senator Ervin, thousands of his fervent adherents are almost tempestuous as they leap to explain: "Senator Sam was one of the most admired, respected, and trusted men on earth, long, long before anyone ever heard of Watergate."

Among some of the Senator's fans, and that's what these "Sam Ervin folks" are, there is almost an implied resentment that many in the television audience are "Johnnies-come-lately." Perhaps, that's why one gets the impression, at times, that Sam Ervin's highly personalized legions indict vast multitudes for sins of omission.

In a word, the national and international television audience is tardy learning what Ervin's legions already knew: Here is a man of enormous decency, tremendous character, fine intellect, marvelous humanity, and delightful wit. And that is precisely why one hears people from one end of North Carolina to the other saying, "Hell, we could have told you about Senator Ervin all along."

Regardless of the literary predelections of these Tar Heels, thousands turn, in essence, to a couplet from Robert Frost:

"They would not find me changed from him
    they knew,
Only more sure of all I thought I was true."

No literary critic has written a better summary of Robert Frost, and if Frost's couplet seeks a permanent home, it finds a lovely, viable dwelling-place in the heart and soul of this strong, gentle man from the North Carolina hill country.

Obviously, most of the statistical facts about Sam Ervin are known widely by now: A lawyer, born to a lawyer, "straight from Abraham's bosom," he attended the University of North Carolina and the Harvard Law School. During World War I he was wounded twice, and, for "conspicuous gallantry," he was awarded the Distinguished Service Cross, the nation's second highest medal for military valor.

Since, and even before, he attained his law degree in 1922, honors have sought Sam Ervin, rather than the other way around. This all started when he was a Harvard law student. Without his own knowledge of what was occurring back home, he was nominated by the Democrats of Burke County, (and elected, subsequently) for the North Carolina legislature.

(It was during the volatile 1925 session of the legislature that the emotional "monkey-law" issue swept into North Carolina from Tennessee, and elsewhere. Ervin helped to save North Carolina for academic freedom and sanity by saying, off-the-cuff: "Only one good thing can come from this. The monkeys in the jungle will be pleased to know that the North Carolina legislature has absolved them for any responsibility for humanity, in general, and for the North Carolina legislature, in particular.")

After three terms in the legislature (every other year for a period of around 120 days), Ervin concentrated on practicing law with his father. He says now: "It was from him that I got the feeling that the freedom of the individual — no matter how lowly he is — is fundamental." Although few men have ever been happier in their chosen professions, Ervin allowed himself to be tapped for county judge in 1935, and in 1937 he accepted appointment to North Carolina's Superior Court. Then in 1948 he was asked to become a member of North Carolina's ultimate tribunal, the Supreme Court. He served as Supreme Court justice for six years. His intention, he said, was to "write decisions that didn't need interpretations."

Most of his friends considered that Sam Ervin "was set for life" as a Supreme Court justice. Then when Senator Clyde R. Hoey died in 1954, Governor William Umstead persuaded Ervin to go to the United States Senate.

In the days before Watergate, Ervin worked assiduously, but quietly, to revise the Code of Military Justice. (It was Ervin's contention that many servicemen were given severe discipline in lieu of justice.) He led the reform of the bail system, the one that gives judges the authority to release men too poor to put up bail but ones who are likely to appear for trial. Long before Watergate, he came down hard on various governmental surveillances of individual citizens, and he obtained passage of the bill that limits the use of lie-detector tests in screening federal employees. And, as is generally known, he was among the first Senators to speak out against indiscriminate wire-tapping.

If the public record is a viable portion of history rendered and of history in the making, it is impossible to know Sam Ervin and not be impressed with the man's almost limitless humanity, his sense of decency and fair play. It was the Sam Ervins of this world whom John Dryden had in mind when he wrote, "His tribe were God Almighty's gentlemen." No one wears the grand old appellation, "gentleman," better. To indicate the measure of the man, and to indicate something of their own feeling about him, his adherents turn twice to Browning, one of the Senator's favorites. One passage is in "Andrea del Sarto: "Ah, but a man's reach should exceed his grasp/Or what's a heaven for?"

And ultimately, without being at all fulsome, they turn to the "Epilogue" to *Asolando:*

> "One who never turned his back but marched
> breast forward,
> Never doubted clouds would break,
> Never dreamed, though right were worsted,
> wrong would triumph,
> Held we fall to rise, are baffled to fight better,
> sleep to wake."

In addition to expressing their profound gratitude to Senator Sam Ervin, Jr., the co-authors of this interview wish to express their gratitude and love to Carla Schiller Butler and to Marguerite Laughridge Stem.

Throughout this interview, the word "interviewer," rather than "interviewers," is used for the obvious purposes of clarity, cohesion, and mobility, and to obviate the cumbersome "we" or "us."

SENATOR SAM ERVIN'S

Best Stories

I

Interviewer: Senator, your smile is as impish as the wind that's courting your lovely azaleas. Have you just read something amusing in that newspaper in your lap?

Ervin: I just read (April 12, 1973) that an undertaker in London opened a coffin to embalm a woman when he heard her snoring loudly.

Interviewer: I suppose the London lady's feelings are about the same Mark Twain had when the newspaper incorrectly reported his death, and he sent the wire: "Your report of my death is somewhat exaggerated."

Ervin: That's it. And I was thinking that many of us have a dramatic, or morbid, desire, a hangup, in today's parlance, to come back from the other side and hear what folks say about us. And your mentioning Mark Twain reminds me that Tom Sawyer, Huck Finn, and Joe Harper are about the only ones who ever heard their own funeral services, the time the three were supposed to have drowned and their bodies never found, in *Tom Sawyer*.

Interviewer: Some of us would probably be astonished at some of the people who came to grieve us, whom we certainly hadn't counted on, and appalled, mad as hell, that some whom we'd put down as sack cloth and ashes mourners didn't show up, because of bad weather or the press of business.,

Ervin: I guess it's just as well that things are as they are. Many years ago this fellow over in Mitchell County died, and he was the sort of man people used to say "wasn't worth hell room in August," that anybody could take a Barlow knife and whittle a better specimen of humanity out of a piece of shingle.

Anyway, the widow and her seven or eight children were sitting at the services as this country preacher really poured it on in his oration. You know the kind of fulsome farewell that preachers used to think they had to give. The preacher piled on accolade after accolade, and at the apogee of his paeans, the widow, completely puzzled and amazed, grabbed her oldest boy by the collar and whispered, none too softly: "Willie, run yonder and be sure it's your Pa in that coffin."

Interviewer: Maybe that's the sort of thing naughty Oscar Wilde had in mind when he wrote, "When the gods wish to punish us they answer our prayers."

Ervin: That reminds me of the time when Woodrow Wilson was so desperately sick, partially paralyzed, and the U.S. Senate sent Senator Albert Fall, who went to prison later on in the Teapot Dome scandal, to investigate Wilson's capacity to continue as President. They let old Fall into Wilson's sick room. Fall put on a sort of Uriah Heep show of mock sympathy, and as he left he said unctuously, "Mr. President, I want you to know the Senate is praying for you."

Quick as a flash, Wilson turned his head toward Fall and asked, "Which way, Senator, which way, Senator?"

Interviewer: Senator, I see an open volume of Kipling's poems on your library desk there. Do you like his poetry?

Ervin: Very much. He's been a favorite of mine for years. I think he always said something, and usually he put his thoughts in memorable language.

Interviewer: Did you know his first name was Joseph, Joseph Rudyard Kipling?

Ervin: If so, I've forgotten it, but in spite of what Shakespeare said about a rose smelling as sweet by any other name, it's mighty hard to imagine someone named "Joseph," or someone called "Joe," being the author of "Gunga Din," or "If," or "Tomlinson," or *Kim*?

Interviewer: That would be about as anachronistic as Judge Samuel J. Ervin, Jr. or Senator Samuel.

Ervin: Yes, and the man who rode to warn about the British has to be Paul Revere and not Appolinaire Rivoire, which I believe was his Christian name, and it's difficult to conceive of Thomas W. Wilson as President, although you know Woodrow was actually his middle name.

Interviewer: Yes siree, and it's little short of impossible to ascribe "A Night at an Inn" and those other eerie, wondrously gripping and plausible melodramas to someone named Plunkett. But as you know, Senator, Lord Dunsany, whose plays and poems we both admire, was really named Edward John Moreton Drax Plunkett.

Ervin: I believe it was Samuel Johnson who wrote of Charles XII, of Sweden, who, after a brilliant military career, a career of really unparalleled brilliance, was killed in a very minor engagement, and is completely forgotten except by a few historians of minutiae: "He

3

left a name at which the world grew pale,/To point a moral, or adorn a tale."

Interviewer: Back to Kipling for a minute, Senator. I should imagine that you like his rollicking stanza: "Two things greater than all things are/The first is women and the second is war./And since we know not how war may prove,/Heart of my heart, let us speak of love."

Ervin: That's right on the mark. Kipling started that poem with "Four things greater than all things are." And the four chief occupations of man were horses, cards, women and war. Then, as you say, he got it down to women and war.

Interviewer: You have some favorite story from the days back in World War I when you served with Company I, 28th Infantry, and were twice wounded?

Ervin: In the early days of the war General Beaumont T. Buck was stationed in Texas. He was working in his flowers one Saturday, wearing an open-neck shirt, without any insigniae, and his army breeches and leather boots. These two draftees came by, and one of them asked General Buck for a match, which he supplied.

The General started talking with the boys and it was apparent that they disliked sergeants more than anything they had encountered in the army. The General asked how long the two boys had been in the army and they told him two weeks. Then one of the recruits asked General Buck how long he had been in the army and he replied, "Thirty years."

One of the boys said, "Well, you must be a sergeant by now?" When the General said "No," one of the boys replied, "Well, you must be a corporal by now?"

When the General said "No," again, one of the draftees spoke up, "If you've been in the army for thirty years and haven't made corporal by now, you must be dumb as hell."

Interviewer: General Gatley, whom you will remember, of the 30th Division, the Old Hickory Division, had the reputation of being the most profane man in the A.E.F.

Ervin: Yes, and I believe he was the father of the movie actress, the old star, Ann Harding.

Interviewer: Yes sir, he was. Well, this single mule was pulling a cart, or some small vehicle, up a hill, some incline in France. The mule kept looking down the incline, lost his balance, fell off the cliff and broke his neck. General Gatley who was standing there, hands on hips, watching the whole thing, snarled: "Serves you right, you scenery-loving son-of-a-bitch."

Ervin: That story seems to be completely authentic. And by the way, the derogation General Gatley applied to the mule may have appeared in formal literature first in *King Lear*, where Shakespeare calls the man, "The son and heir of a mongrel bitch."

Interviewer: And, unfortunately, the tribe hasn't disappeared, although we sort of switch it around today. A little while ago you quoted Samuel Johnson. Boswell said: "It is well known that there was formerly a rude custom for those who were sailing on the Thames to accost each other, as they passed, in the most abusive language they could invent, generally, however, with as much satirical humor as they could invent."

One day when Johnson was on the river a fellow yelled to him that his wife was a bawd, and Johnson answered with his classic retort, "Sir, your wife, under pretense of keeping a bawdy-house, is a receiver of stolen goods."

Ervin: Some years ago there were some scandals, shortages, in the North Carolina Revenue Department. By today's standards, there wasn't a whole lot of money involved, but many employees of the Revenue Department were indicted and the papers were filled with the stories for a long time. Anyway, according to the story that was prevalent, this fellow from one of the Eastern counties was in Raleigh and he ran into a hometown man on Fayetteville Street.

The older man said: "Bill, what are you doing here in Raleigh?"

Bill replied: "I got a paying job. I'm working."

"Well, all right, but where do you work?"

Bill took the older man down a side street and whispered: "I'm employed at the Revenue Department, but my folks think I'm playing the piano in a sporting-house, and if you go back home and tell them the truth, I'll be disgraced, ruined for life."

Interviewer: Senator, you'll recall that the late W.J. Brogden, that brilliant jurist and wonderful humanitarian, who didn't like golf, especially, told the story about the professional golfer, in the old days, who wrote his folks he had been promoted from helper to first-assistant to a man who gutted fish.

Ervin: Brogden was one of the greatest lawyers and quickest wits I ever knew. When he was on the State Supreme Court, the Harward case, an extremely celebrated matter, went up to the higher court on appeal from the Superior Court. This was a most complex matter and Justice Brogden and his associates studied the case for a lengthy period. While the court was still deliberating, Brogden was accosted on the streets of Durham by some officious, ill-mannered man who asked:

"When are you birds," — get that, "birds" — "going to rule on the Harward case?"

Brodgen replied: "I can't tell you that but I can explain it with a companion story. This fellow was riding along the highway when he saw a rope, just the end of a rope, with nothing on it, dangling from an abandoned well. There was nothing in the field but the abandoned well, and the man was so obsessed with curiosity he got out of his car, walked across the old field and looked down into the bottom of the well. The well was dry, and lo and behold, he saw his best friend sitting down there playing the rope.

With complete astonishment he blurted out, "Why, John Jones, what in the world are you doing sitting in the bottom of that old well?"

Came the reply, "None of your damned business, you confounded busy-body, and if you weren't such a good friend of mine I wouldn't tell you that much."

Interviewer: Senator Sam, the Watergate investigation has made your name and your face vibrant in virtually every literate household in the land, but as you sit here this rare spring morning in your spacious, lovely library, in your charming home, you don't resemble the stereotype of the crusading Senator. Instead, you call up Hubert Humphrey's two-line biography: "In the Senate we all call him the 'Judge.' He knows more law and more good stories than anyone in Washington, than anyone anywhere."

II

Ervin: Well, sitting here this morning swapping yarns with you boys, talking about poetry, and looking at the azaleas, I don't feel especially toga-like.

Interviewer: When my love-affair with you began, you were a lawyer, a Superior Court judge, not a Senator, not a national figure. And as John Heywood said in one of his 17th century proverbs, "Much water goeth by the mill that the miller knoweth not of."

What I mean is that the courthouse and the political stump used to be almost synonymous with outrageous men, with their salty stories, and warts-and-all convolutions. Today, one hardly ever hears any good courthouse or political stories, and the few one does hear could apply just as easily to some other institution. What's caused this enormous change, what I call a tragic change?

Ervin: It's the inevitable by-product, or casualty, from your point of view, of the enormous sweep from insular to urban society. The old gregarious homogeneity of provincial days has been replaced by a sort of standardized approach to life. And, of course, we don't turn to the courthouse and the political hustings for amusement and diversion today because we are almost inundated with entertainments and amusements, professional and amateur athletics, golf, tennis, television, boating, just dozens and dozens of participatory and spectator sports and activities.

Interviewer: There's no damned humor or saltiness in Perry Mason, Owen Marshall and the others. They seem to go about practicing law the way one of these automatic machines sets up the knocked down pens in a bowling parlor, alley, I mean.

Ervin: You give yourself away with "parlor." I believe parlor comes from the Middle Latin "parlatorium," originally, and it meant a talking room. Of course, we used to have funeral parlors, cocktail parlors, pool parlors, parlor cars on trains — all sorts of parlors. But to get back to your question, the courthouse was far more than a place in which justice was dispensed, deeds recorded, and wills probated when I began practicing law.

There were few recorders' courts, and most counties had a two-weeks' term of Superior Court four times a year, in spring, summer, fall, and winter. People from the rural sections filled the local hotel and boarding-houses during each term of court. And "city" homes were opened to rural relatives and friends who came to town for the festivities.

In provincial days, court week, or "coat" week, as most Tar Heels called it, was a sort of bucolic Mardi Gras. All sorts of vendors hawked all sorts of wares. "Dog and Pony" shows performed on the court house lawn, and the old medicine show always came to town.

Interviewer: I saw several medicine shows, myself,

Senator, and they were a sight to behold. The three or four musicians played and danced on the tail-gate of the wagon to whip up a crowd. Then the "Doc," the medicine show man, came out in his beaver hat and fancy duds to sell his magic elixirs.

Ervin: That's it, exactly, and he usually said he got his secret formula from some Zulu chieftan who lived to be at least a hundred and fifty, taking the same stuff.

Interviewer: Right on, Senator. The "Doc" had been everywhere, seen everything. He had done everything from going with Peary to the North Pole to being Bob Fitzsimmons' sparring partner. As Edwin Arlington Robinson said in one of his poems, the "Doc" really "glittered when he walked," and he sparkled when he talked.

Ervin: Yes, and the amazing thing is that virtually everyone knew the "Doc" was a complete fraud. He probably hadn't been any closer to the North Pole than southside Virginia. And people knew the medicine was bellywash, but buying a bottle was a small premium to pay for hearing the musicians, seeing them clog dance, and listening to the "Doc's" hypnotic verbiage.

Interviewer: As I recall, the imperial "Doc's" elixirs and potions were always cracked up to be "good for man or beast," and just as efficacious on the outside of the human or animal's body as inside it?

Ervin: Precisely. Most of the people in the crowd were farmers, or people who owned animals, and, according to the "Doc," the purchaser could treat himself, inside and outside, and his mule, inside and outside, from the same bottle of medicine.

Interviewer: I'd hate like hell to try to get a mule to drink from a bottle or to get medicine down his throat with a spoon.

Ervin: As Josh Billings put it, "A ·mule don't kick according to no rules."

Interviewer: I realize this is a deviation, from the great days of "coat" week, to which we shall return shortly, but several times recently on national television and in national publications you have referred to Josh Billings. That was a pseudonym, wasn't it, Senator?

Ervin: Absolutely. Josh Billings was the pen name of Henry Wheeler Shaw, who lived from eighteen hundred and eighteen to eighteen eighty-five. I suppose you'd call him a dialect humorist.

Interviewer: That was a popular device, with nineteenth century humorists, using a pseudonym, and Charles Farrar Browne, who wrote under the name of "Artemus Ward," may have been the first in the line of the genre.

Ervin: And postal officials, especially postmasters, acquired the generic nickname "Nasby" from the writings of David Ross Locke who signed his satirical newspaper articles as "The Rev. Petroleum Vesuvius Nasby, Postmaster at Confedrit X Roads, which is in the state of Kentucky."

The writer, Locke, or Nasby, pretended to be a Negro-hating office-seeker who was determined to get the job of postmaster at "Confedrit X Roads, Ky." His comic writings saddled "Nasby" on political postmasters for a long time, long after Locke, or Nasby, died in eighteen eighty-eight. And "Nasby" came to mean any venal person who held office as a sinecure, just for the salary or what he could knock down.

Interviewer: Yes sir, and he gave the same lecture, "Cursed Be Canaan," around twenty-five hundred different times. The lecture always began with the sentence, "We are all descended from ancestors."

Ervin: George Washington Harris, who called himself Sut Lovingood, was another humorist with a tremendous following, another who wrote in dialect. Old Sut wrote a couplet about the Yankee's big foot, something that Dean Samuel Fox Mordecai, of the Trinity and Duke Law School, liked to quote.

Interviewer: How does it go?

Ervin: "Sut Lovingood said about his foot, I remembered it this minute, /'Twere the longest thing I ever saw not to have guts in it."

Interviewer: Well, Sut Lovingood anticipated today's fashion with all the barefoot high school and college students who walk the sidewalks without shoes. They do not leave footprints on the sands of time, but they certainly make the sidewalk sound as if a million plumbers'-helpers are going simultaneously.

Ervin: (Laughing) Anyway, they will never be bothered by where the shoe pinches them.

Interviewer: I think Plutarch said, "None of you can tell me where the shoe pinches you."

Ervin: Plutarch may have referred to one of the first divorce cases of official record. A Roman divorced his wife to the amazement of his friends who could see no fault in her. The man handed his friends one of his shoes, a brand new pair, and asked if any one of them could tell him where the shoe pinched him.

Interviewer: I suppose the days of "everyday" and "Sunday" shoes are gone forever Senator.

Ervin: Yes, with the ice wagon and the ten cent pack of cigarettes.

In parlous times when there was a wedding in some of

our fine families that were too poor to paint and too proud to whitewash, a little brother might not have any decent shoes to wear to his sister's wedding. So a favorite device was to wrap the little fellow's right big toe in a billowing homemade rag bandage and saturate the rag with turpentine. The little fellow practiced his limp just as the bridesmaids practiced for the wedding. And, when he finally limped down the aisle, he stole the show from bride and groom and all of the handsomely-attired wedding party.

Interviewer: That reminds me, Senator, Bill Arp, one of the most famous of the post-Civil War humorists, told Josephus Daniels his name was actually Bill "Earp," that his people moved from Eastern North Carolina to Georgia, somewhat precipitately, packed hastily, and didn't have time to take that capital"E" along to the new home in Georgia. As you know, "Earp" has always been pronounced "Arp" in Eastern Carolina, although it is called "Erp" out west, with Wyatt Earp and his gun-toting brothers.

Ervin: That's sort of like "Tieless Joe" Tolbert, long a Republican leader in South Carolina, who lived until fairly recently, and never wore a necktie because, as he explained, "I don't never take nothing I don't need, nothing extra."

And there was a Louisiana lawyer who never wore a tie. Most of his practice was restricted to magistrates' courts, and the absence of the tie didn't create any particular stir. But one day he had a case in the circuit court, which his opponent appealed to the state supreme court.

His friends told him he simply had to wear a tie when he appeared before the supreme court at Baton Rouge,

13

that appearing before that august tribunal tieless would be a frightful affront. But, he explained, testily, "I don't put on no dog here, and I'm not going to put on any dog in Baton Rouge."

Well, he went down and argued his case, and after five or six weeks he got a copy of the opinion and it was against his client. He studied the opinion as best he could, and the more he studied it, the more puzzled he became. He told his friends he was going to Baton Rouge, on the train, of course, and ask the chief justice if he lost his case because he didn't wear a tie.

He saw the chief justice, identified himself and his case, and said: "Well, Judge, I make it a habit never to wear a necktie, and my friends warned me I ought to wear one in your court. So, I have come down here to find out whether your court decided against me because I wasn't wearing a tie when I argued the case before you."

The chief justice replied, somewhat indignantly, "Of course not. Your not wearing a tie had nothing to do with the case."

Then the lawyer said: "Well, Judge, I didn't know. I've read your opinion many times over, and that reason would have been far better than any reason you gave in your opinion, ruling against my client."

Interviewer: I suppose today's psychologist would say going tieless was a form of reverse snobbery. I'm sure you agree that many people today make a fetish of contrived simplicity. I'll tell you a true story about one of the greatest of the modern American poets, a gentleman who attained an incredible age, and died within the past few years.

His lustrous white hair was always in a massive

14

disarray, and this lady, a good writer herself, said of the patriarch: "The old so and so sat in front of the mirror for two hours combing his hair so that it would look as if it had never been combed."

Ervin: Someone said, "Affected simplicity is a subtle form of imposture."

Interviewer: I believe that was La Rochefoucauld, in one of his *Maxims,* and Dickens wrote, in *Martin Chuzzlewit*, I think, "There is a simplicity of cunning no less than a simplicity of innoncence."

III

But back to "coat" week, Senator. Just what did the phrase, "Tuesday of Court Week," or actually "Chewsday of coat week" mean? For example, I remember the story about the old Tar Heel who had hardly been out of his native Granville County. Then one time he had to go to Washington, D.C., or Washington City, as most of our folks used to call it.

He rode the night train up to Washington, got off at the Union Station, near the Capitol, saw the crowds of people and the innumerable vehicles, and exclaimed, in complete consternation, "Good God, is this here 'Chewsday of coat week?' "

Ervin: Well, it was completely natural for your old fellow to imagine no such crowd of people would be on the streets anywhere unless superior court was in session. The big drama always started on the first Tuesday of the quarterly two-weeks' term. On Monday, the judge presiding charged the grand jury, and he went over the docket with the lawyers. He also heard excuses from those called to jury duty who were sick or involved in something that precluded jury duty. So, the first Monday

16

was spent in rudimentary matters. That meant that the big drama, the trying of cases, started on Tuesday, and this was what attracted all those people, what they came to see and to hear. And, not just incidentally, most folks did say "Chewsday."

Interviewer: I guess I still do, and I also say "aint," as in "my Aunt Lucy."

Ervin: True enough, James Mason, of Virginia, an aristocrat of all Old Dominion aristocrats, always referred to himself as "Jeems." He married a member of the illustrious Chew family of Philadelphia and he always said he married a "Chaw."

Interviewer: What did the audience like best, the examination of witnesses, the cross-examination, or the speeches to the jury?

Ervin: They liked all of it, and some incredible things happened, completely unexpectedly. Years ago a woman was riding the train. When she reached her station, she said the porter picked up the stool, the little trick passengers used to step from the bottom step of the coach to the ground.

She went sprawling down on the ground, which, as you remember, was packed with cinders at many station yards. She was examined by her local physician who said the fall had permanently injured one of her female organs and that this injury would preclude bearing children.

The judge presiding was old Judge Charles M. Cooke, of Franklin County, one of the last of the Confederate veteran lawyers, and a man who held court well into this century. In many respects, Judge Cooke, whom I knew, was the most complete individual in the state's history. Well, it was necessary, at some point in the trial, to read back some of the testimony, and the court stenographer was reading the doctor's testimony, in which he named the female organ that was injured in the fall.

She looked up at Judge Cooke and asked: "How do you spell that, Judge?"

"Hell, I don't know," he snarled. "You ought to know. You got one and I ain't."

Interviewer: Didn't many individual lawyers have trememdous local followings?

Ervin: They certainly did. The lawyers of that era knew virtually everyone in the county, their prejudices, religious affiliations, what made them mad, and what made them sympathetic, and a good lawyer tried to salt one or two people of whom he had intimate knowledge on the jury. Back then lawyers appeared at all sorts of rural functions — fish fries, family reunions, homecomings, funerals, and "dinners-on-the-ground." All the churches had dinners-on-the-grounds as a vital part of their summer revivals. You still see eating benches on the lawns of some rural churches today.

In connection with this, former Chancellor Bob House, of U.N.C., says he ate at so many dinners on the ground as a boy in Halifax County he never sees a piece of fried chicken today, or a piece of chess pie, without expecting to have a conviction of original sin . . .

Lawyers appeared in amateur theatricals and spelling bees all over the county, and they made speeches at hundreds of various occasions. You have to remember that there were no amplifiers and most of the speeches were made outdoors, frequently against the wind. Of necessity some fine speaking voices were developed. You don't get the same thing today speaking with amplifiers, and on radio and T.V.

Many lawyers picked out one man on the jury and sort of made their speech to him. If he liked classical literature, or fishing, or some facet of nature, the lawyer brought this into his speech.

Interviewer: You mean Senator, that much of a trial lawyer's success was predicated on his own knowledge of the whimsicalities and caprices of individual jurors?

Ervin: That's exactly right. When I was a young lawyer I was representing a man who was charged with rape. I thought I put up a powerful argument, and I was delighted when the jury hung and the judge declared a mistrial. I found out that an old mountaineer by the name of Wilson had hung the jury.

A few weeks after the trial, Mr. Wilson was in my office about some civil matter. I was interested to know what had caused him to vote not guilty, and I asked him if he was impressed most by the testimony, or my speech to the jury, or by the judge's charge to the jury.

The old man replied "I didn't pay a damn bit of attention to what any witnesses said, to what the damn judge said, or to a damn thing you said, boy."

"Then why did you vote 'not guilty'?"

Because, goddamit, it can't be done. Haven't I tried it dozens of times?

Interviewer: A lawyer in Granville County won a rape case solely on the basis of semantics.

Ervin: How did that happen?

Interviewer: A girl testified she had been raped due to fear for her life. She testified that the defendant threw her down in a tobacco field and threatened her with a pocketknife. Now, shortly before this, the girl had worked in a cafe in Raleigh or Durham for a while and had picked up some "city" phrases.

19

The defendant's lawyer on cross examination asked her to tell exactly what had happened and she replied: "He held his pocketknife to my throat and said, 'If you don't remove your underthings, I am going to kill you.'"

The defendant's lawyer asked her the same question three or four times, phrasing it slightly differently each time, and, invariably, she used the same phrase: "If you don't remove your underthings, I am going to kill you."

The defendant was uneducated and not very bright. His lawyer placed him on the stand and mercilessly exposed the poor boy's ignorance. The late Henry Stevens, of Warsaw, N.C., was presiding and the lawyer argued to Judge Stevens that never in his life had this poor boy thought or spoken in terms of "remove" or "underthings."

"No, your Honor, if he had said anything he would have said, "Gal, take them damn drawers off." The lawyer argued that if the girl lied about one thing in the case she probably lied about the whole thing.

Ervin: My guess is Henry agreed with the lawyer.

Interviewer: Yes sir, he certainly did.

Ervin: As you may know, Henry, Judge Stevens, was national commander of the American Legion, and I believe he is the youngest man ever to hold that honor.

Interviewer: I believe it was Judge Stevens who presided at an unusual bastardy trial. This fairly affluent farmer, a man of sixty-two, was indicted by a young single girl of twenty-two who swore he was the father of her illegitimate child.

The sixty-two year old defendant had two lawyers, one about his age and one much younger. The younger attorney investigated the prosecuting witness's background thoroughly. He established beyond

20

peradventure that the girl was notoriously promiscuous, ran around with many boys her own age, that in conjunction with the actual father of her baby she was like the rabbit that ran through the briar patch and couldn't say just which briar scratched it. So, the young lawyer wanted to establish this in court, and impeach the girl's reputation.

Ervin: That can be dangerous because lots of juries tend to sympathize with a woman, especially if they get the idea somebody is picking on her.

Interviewer: That's what the older lawyer said. He said to his eager young associate: "We both know damn well this gal tagged our client because he has some money, and those young boys she's been running around with don't have enough money, among them, to buy a sack of Bull Durham. Now, if you don't mind too much, let's don't try to impeach her character. Just sort of humor me and my way and let's see what happens."

The younger said that was all right, and when they got down to picking the jury the older lawyer excused several people until he got four or five men in the box about his age and about the age of the defendant.

Ervin: This was before women started serving on juries in North Carolina?

Interviewer: Yes sir, I believe it was. The girl swore the defendant was the father of her child. The older lawyer didn't ask her any indicting questions, but the younger lawyer just had to ask how she could be so sure.

The girl looked at the young lawyer as if he were the village idiot. Then she said, almost incredulously: "Mister, don't you know a girl can always tell when she lets her sweetness down?"

When the defendant testified he admitted, freely, on

21

direct examination that he had intimate relations with the girl. The older lawyer asked if the defendant could remember any specific dates, fix the time definitely, and the defendant answered that he remembered having intercourse with the girl on October twenty-second.

Ervin: That was about nine months before the baby was born?

Interviewer: Yes sir. He said he knew it was October twenty-second because he came to town early that morning with a big load of tobacco, that he still had the bill-of-sale. And he also remembered going to Raleigh that same night to the State Fair.

The older lawyer said, "Well, just go ahead and tell us in your own words what happened that day."

The defendant said he got up about five o'clock that morning, packed his tobacco on his truck, had breakfast and so on. The older lawyer asked; "What did you eat for breakfast?"

Of course, private prosecution objected that what the man ate for breakfast was irrelevant. But the older lawyer said, gently enough, "If your Honor pleases, we are trying to put a whole day's events into chronological order, and a day, like a battle or a poem, has to have a proper beginning, middle, and end. Then he quoted a couplet from Alexander Pope: "What dire offence from am'rous causes springs,/What mighty contests rise from trivial things."

The judge, and I think it was Henry Stevens, said it might be somewhat irrelevant but he could see no harm in the man's telling how the day started, what he ate for breakfast.

The defendant said he ate some raw oysters, dry cereal with a banana on it, and brains and eggs. The old lawyer asked if he usually stuck to this same diet, and the man said he did, although he might have oyster soup instead of raw oysters in cold weather.

In describing the remainder of the day he said he had relations with the girl about nine o'clock that morning, while he waited for his tobacco to be sold, and that he had intimate relations again with her the same afternoon, after his tobacco was sold and before he went to Raleigh to the fair.

Cross-examination was bland, almost negligible; and when the sixty-two year old defendant got ready to leave the witness stand, the old lawyer escorted him back to the counsels' table the way the Old Guard might have escorted Napoleon.

The older men on the jury were about ten feet tall, and the way their chests swelled it's a wonder they didn't shoot the buttons from their shirts all over the courthouse. The old lawyer beamed as if he just crossed the Delaware with George Washington, and the judge, certainly a middle-aged man at the time, had such a sparkle in his eyes they could have been used for warning signals in that big lighthouse down at Cape Hatteras.

The jury hung, the same as yours in the rape case, Senator, and when the court room began to empty, one of the late jurors, a wealthy, aristocratic gentleman, a huge landowner of around sixty-five, stood chatting and smoking with the old lawyer.

This wonderful example of landed gentry pulled a little scrap of paper from a vest pocket and said: "Let's see, your client says he starts off with dry cereal and a banana."

The judge almost leaped from the bench, where he

was fiddling with some papers. When he joined the juror and the lawyer he reached under his robe, pulled out a piece of paper, and said: "No, by God, gentlemen. He said he starts with raw oysters and then has the cereal and banana and then the brains and eggs."

The lawyer quoted a line from Lord Byron, from *Don Juan:* "Oysters are amatory food."

Ervin: I understand that in some species of oysters the sexes are separate and in some the sexes are united in the same oyster. This must lead to complications of such an astounding nature mere human beings should refrain from comment about their own problems.

Interviewer: I can just hear one half of an oyster's saying to the other half: "No, not tonight. I've been ironing all day."

Ervin: A little to one side, someone once said, "A man may as well open an oyster without a knife, as a lawyer's mouth without a fee."

And, by the way, ginseng, which grows abundantly up here, was cracked-up to have the same magical properties.

Interviewer: I think I remember some references to ginseng in William Byrd's secret diary, but I believe his references were to ginseng roots and camomile flowers for rudimentary family illnesses. But, Senator, isn't it a historical fact that ginseng was vital in opening trade between this country and China?

Ervin: Absolutely. The root flourished in China but the Chinese used it so extensively as an aphrodisiac the going price of the root became exorbitant. Then the imperial Chinese government forbade any gathering of the root, because the supply was so short, and early in the nineteenth century the Chinese began to import

24

ginseng from America.

A lot of this was picked here in our mountains and several crude mills for drying and shipping ginseng were started in some of the mountain counties. Insofar as I can tell, most of it was shipped on to China.

Interviewer: Good Lord, do you mean we are somewhat to blame for China's enormous population?"

Ervin: I suppose you could make such an argument, humorously, facetiously, but I believe there is general scientific agreement that any value from ginseng was purely psychic. Just the same, Daniel Boone gathered "sang," as it was called, and in seventeen eighty-eight he took fifteen tons of the stuff up the Ohio for shipment to Philadelphia. Boone gathered it in Kentucky and western Virginia, and some of it may have ended up in China.

Interviewer: That's entirely possible. I read somewhere that the *Empress of China,* which sailed in seventeen eighty-four, and is supposed to be the first American ship to reach China, carried a large cargo of ginseng. So, I assume the next ships to China did, too.

Ervin, suddenly focusing on interviewer's umbrella which had fallen to the floor, somewhat clatteringly: They used to tell this story about Mr. Frank Watson, a white-bearded, truly eloquent lawyer, of Burnsville, who lived until fairly recently.

"Colonel" Watson, as this handsome-distinguished-looking man was called, was walking along one fine spring day, when there wasn't a dark cloud in the sky, carrying a handsome umbrella, using it as a man might use a cane or a swagger stick.

Some wiseacre who was lounging around the courthouse square hailed him: "Colonel Watson, whatchu doing toting a umbrella when the sun's a-shining so bright?"

Without even checking his stride, Mr. Watson said over his shoulder, "Young man, any damned fool can carry an umbrella when it's raining."

Interviewer: You remember that nutty story about the Carolina professor who was so absent-minded he put his umbrella in bed with his wife and then stood in the corner all night?

Ervin: Yes, I heard that one when I was an undergraduate at Carolina. A while back, we were talking about Judge Henry Stevens. Henry and some of the other judges and lawyers liked the story about the small-town preacher who lost his handsome umbrella. This umbrella, a most ornate one, was extra special, had been given the minister by a previous congregation. One day he told the chairman of his board of stewards that someone had stolen his valuable umbrella, and he asked for advice on the best means of recovering it.

The steward, a wise old merchant, scratched his head, beamed and said: "Here's the solution. This coming Sunday you just preach a powerful sermon on the Ten Commandments, and when you get to the one that says 'Thou shall not steal,' you really bear down, let out all the stops. My guess is that the guilty person will return your umbrella to your study when you are out."

The next Sunday morning the preacher really turned loose bearing down on the Ten Commandments, but he quit cold before he got to "Thou shall not steal." The puzzled steward waited for the preacher after the service: "Look here, parson, you didn't say a word about 'Thou shall not steal.' What happened?"

The preacher, looking as hacked as what people used

to call a suck-egg-dog, replied meekly: "Well, it's like this. When I got to the commandment that says 'Thou shall not commit adultery,' I remembered where I had left my umbrella."

Interviewer: That reminds me of Charles Bowen's rhymed dictim:

"The rain it raineth on the just
And also on the unjust fella:
But chiefly on the just, because
The unjust steals the just's umbrella."

I understand umbrellas were the first status-symbols, Senator, that they were used, as sunshades, in China. Egypt, and Mesopotamia as early as the 12th century B.C. Very few people could afford umbrellas, and they were the mark of royalty. The ancient ruler, Ava, called himself, officially, "The King of White Elephants and the Lord of twenty-four umbrellas."

Ervin: Adolf Hitler drew a most erroneous conclusion from the fact that Neville Chamberlain carried an umbrella at Munich, always carried something Hitler considered so effete as an umbrella, then the British people would be too feckless to resist him.

Interviewer: Many Americans had a hard time believing Gene Tunney, father of your fellow Senator, John Tunney, from California, could beat Jack Dempsey because some sports writers saw Gene Tunney reading Shakespeare at his training camp.

Anyhow, a while back you were talking about the great days of the justice of the peace's courts, when few courts of record existed in North Carolina. Wasn't court held wherever the justice of peace did business or

27

worked?

Ervin: Oh, my goodness, yes. Every township had at least one, in horse-and-buggy days, and even afterwards in sparsely-populated places. Sometimes the magistrate, the "Squire," ran a country store, and his bench was a counter in the store. The testimony, the whole proceedings, might be interrupted a dozen times while the magistrate rolled out a barrel of flour for a customer, or drew a gallon of molasses or kerosene oil, measured and cut off some dress goods for a lady, or sold some child a penny's worth of candy.

Interviewer: I take it, Senator, they were not experts in the rules of evidence, that they held court the way the World War I pilots said they flew airplanes, "By the seats of their pants."

Ervin: Many were not encumbered with legal training. One time a young mountain lawyer, whose zeal may have surpassed his common sense, at that precise juncture, lost a case in a J.P. court, in a country store, and after the adjourment of court, when the magistrate's Bible was off the "bench" and the checker-board was back on the counter, the young lawyer, in a spirit of retaliation, suggested strongly that the squire had received improper *scire facais* fees.

Obviously, the very sound of "scirefacias" galvanized everyone in the store. The magistrate spat a stream of tobacco juice into his cuspidor, wiped beads of sudden, nervous sweat from his face, and turned to a man standing by: "George, you better ride like hell and get Doc Roberts so he can vaccinate the whole damn township.

Interviewer: What did the young lawyer really mean?

Ervin: Today "scire facias," what the lawyers

commonly refer to as "sci-fai", means that a bondsman is ordered into court. He must produce the person for whom bond is given, or forfeit the bond. But at the time in the story, district solicitors and magistrates got flat fees of forfeited appearance bonds. Then the legislature changed the law, under the old "School Laws," to a collection of five per cent, instead of a flat fee, on such defaulted bonds. Some of the magistrates didn't know about the change, and that's what the lawyer meant.

Interviewer: That's like the candidate who went around telling folks his opponent's wife was a thespian."

Ervin: Yes, and another lawyer turned to his client in a magistrate's trial and said, somewhat loudly, that his case was *coram non judices.* Whereupon, the startled J.P. exclaimed, "If the poor fellow's in that bad shape, we'll pass the hat and he can have everything that's collected above the costs of the 'coat'."

Interviewer: "Coram non judices" isn't a communicable disease, as the squire assumed?

Ervin: No, it means that a specific court has no jurisdiction, and that any judgment rendered by it is invalid.

Interviewer: The magistrate's ignorance of legal parlance reminds me of something Heine said about Latin: "The Romans would never have found time to conquer the world if they had been obliged to learn Latin first." I guess the old squires adhered to the ancient Scottish proverb, "Show me the man and I'll show you the law."

Ervin: That was certainly true of many of them, and if they never heard this old proverb, "Law and equity are two things which God hath joined together, but which man hath put asunder," they seemed often to put

29

it into concrete practice.

For instance, this justice of the peace wanted to go fishing, although he was trying a case in which there was a lawyer appearing on each side. When the evidence had been presented, he asked the lawyers if they wanted to argue the case. They said they did, and the justice of the peace asked how much time they wanted for arguments. They asked for an hour on each side.

The justice replied, "You gentlemen have a right to do that, and I will let you argue to your hearts' content, but I'm going fishing. When you get through with your speeches, just pick up that book that's lying on my desk, and under it you will find my decision already written out."

Interviewer: A lawyer told me about this true experience from his early days at the bar. He had a case in a magistrate's court, way back in the sticks. When court "convened," the squire was doctoring a sick cow, and court was held in his milk-shed, with the jurist ensconced on a turned over milk bucket.

The lawyer had found a case that was in his favor, one completely parallel to the matter at hand, that had just been decided by the state supreme court. He read the decision to the justice slowly and deliberately.

When he finished, he snapped his book closed and said to the justice, "That's it, Your Honor, Q.E.D., Squire, quod erat demonstratudum."

The squire cogitated, whittled a stick, drummed on the milk bucket, and asked: "Whar does at air coat set?"

"Why, Your Honor, the supreme court sits in Raleigh, our state capital."

"Well 'en, aye, God, at might be the law in Rolly but it shore God ain't the law in Tally Ho Township."

Ervin: Another old justice of the peace was terribly exasperated by the tactics of a young lawyer who was trying his first case. The young lawyer kept bobbing up to exclaim, "I object. You are not proceeding according to law."

When the old magistrate could stand the interruptions no longer, he shouted: "Young man, quit jumping up and saying 'I object. You are not proceeding according to law.' I'll have you understand I am running this court, and the law hasn't got a damn thing to do with it."

IV

Interviewer: That calls up your story about the time Andrew Jackson, in vetoing the act of Congress that created the national bank, inserted a message saying the act was unconstitutional.

Jackson's secretary turned to him: "You can't make that statement in your veto message because a similar act's constitutionality has already been upheld by the Supreme Court, and you are sworn to uphold the Constitution."

"Huh," Jackson snorted," I am sworn to uphold the Constitution as Andy Jackson understands it and interprets it."

And not just incidentally, Senator, didn't one of your ancestors almost end Andrew Jackson's career before it began?

Ervin: That's the accepted story.

Interviewer: May we deviate from the days of the magistrates long enough to hear what happened?

Ervin: The old story is told by that fine historian, Glenn Tucker, of Fairview, North Carolina, in his excellent biography, *Zeb Vance: Champion of Personal*

Freedom, which was published seven or eight years ago.

According to the story, young Jackson's legal resources were restricted to one book, Bacon's *Abridgement,* and everywhere he went he carried a copy of it in his saddlebag, wrapped in brown grocer's paper. It was young Jackson's custom in court, when a close issue developed, to say to the court, "Let's see what Bacon says about this."

In seventeen eighty-eight, at court in Jonesboro, then in North Carolina, but now in Tennessee, Judge Waightstill Avery, a member of the class of seventeen seventy-six at Princeton, decided to break Jackson of his tiresome habit.

Interviewer: How old was Jackson at this time?

Ervin: He was twenty-one years old. Before court one morning Judge Avery removed Bacon's *Abridgement* from Jackson's saddlebag, and he put a piece of real bacon, the same size as the book, in the brown wrapping paper.

That same morning in court when Jackson was nearing the end of a tempestuous plea, he reached into his saddlebag and said triumphantly, "Now, let's see what Bacon says."

Then he untied his package. All the lawyers, court officials, and spectators howled when Jackson held up the greasy piece of hog's back. Enraged, the youngster challenged Avery to a duel. Avery, who seems to have been a fairly strict Presbyterian, was opposed to dueling, but nothing he said could calm Jackson's temper.

In the duel, Jackson fired first. He was supposed to be a crack shot, and although he undoubtedly intended to kill Avery, his bullet merely clipped the older man's ear. Under the rule of the code duello, Jackson, a man of honor, was required to stand at his post docilely while Judge Avery fired. Jackson stood without any flinching, but Avery fired his pistol into the air, advanced, with a broad smile, shook Jackson's hands, both hands, to close the incident forever, and he spared the hot-headed youngster to go ahead to an illustrious career.

Interviewer: Senator, was the Judge's first name, "Waightstill," originally "Wait-Still-Upon-The-Lord?" I've seen that in print.

Ervin: That's a story many people like, but it could be entirely apocryphal.

Interviewer: Before we took that detour to Jonesboro, Senator, we were talking about the ineffectuality of legal oratory on magistrates. Don't you think lawyer's arguments are effective, that they really influence judges and juries?

Ervin: As many times as there are green leaves on those shade trees along the street. The actual examples are too innumerable even to begin to suggest more than an inadequate sampling, but three or four classics that come to mind are Andrew Hamilton's speech in seventeen thirty-three, when he defended John Peter Zanger, the editor, in the first freedom of the press case; Daniel Webster's speech in the matter of the charter of Dartmouth College, when he said, "Dartmouth is small but there are those of us who love it;" and Clarence Darrow's speech, to the judge, when he saved the lives of Loeb and Leopold after they had pled guilty to the kidnapping and murder of young Bobby Franks.

One of the most bizarre examples of effective argument involved a lawyer in one of our mountain counties whose passion for trying cases was matched, even exceeded, by his zeal for the bottle.

Interviewer: What happened, Senator?

Ervin: His habit was to secrete a bottle, or a Mason jar of moonshine, somewhere around the courthouse, or to slip out to his office, which was a door or two from the courthouse. He did this for years, but during the trial of a particular case, he drank too much, so much, in fact, that when he got up to address the jury, he got his side confused with the other side.

He stood there at the jury box giving his own client pluperfect hell for about twenty minutes. Then, it came to him what he was doing. He went to the water cooler, took a refreshing swallow, smiled sweetly, knowingly at the jurors, and said in a clear voice: "Now, gentlemen of the jury, that's what the other side will say about my client when they argue the case to you, but I will now tell you the straight of it."

Interviewer: He won his case?

Ervin: Yes, and it was a matter of complete alcoholic confusion and not cheap theatricals.

Interviewer: Your reference to "Mason jar," for years the standard receptacle for corn or white whiskey in North Carolina, reminds me of a true story. This really affable farmer used to come to town every Saturday night and get drunk. He never bothered anybody, and even when drunk, he was extremely deferential, but now and then he'd start clog-dancing on a street corner or to "testifying," as if he were at a revival or camp-meeting, and the "night policeman" would lock him up until he slept it off.

One Saturday night he started "testifying," sort of like Billy Sunday or Billy Graham going in reverse, and the policeman put him in the bull-ring with several others being detained for petty offenses. He went around the bull-ring introducing himself and shaking hands with the other prisoners. He was the epitome of courtliness until he shook hands with a man who said, "My name is Mason."

The courtly drunk slung Mason's hand down, and sizzled, "If you're the cheap son-of-a-bitch who made them short fruit-jars, you ought to be in a jail."

Ervin: Yes, many men who used to buy moonshine said the alleged quart Mason jar held only a fifth in reality. And your story reminds me of Vice-President Alban Barkley's story of the farmer who came to town one Saturday afternoon, bought a new wagon, hitched his team to it, and then got smashed.

En route home he passed out in the wagon, and some friend who came along drove the wagon off the road into the shade of the woods, unhitched the team and took them to the man's stable. He awakened in the cold, gray dawn, rubbed his eyes, stretched, looked around, surveyed the situation, saw the wagon tongue on the ground, and exclaimed, "One of two things is sure. I either lost a team or found a damn good wagon."

Interviewer: Back to the drunk lawyer, and his unusual jury speech. I have heard that many of the old-time lawyers kept "refreshments" in their offices, behind the big yellow books, the classics, the copies of Robert Burns and Tennyson, but all the drinking wasn't confined to lawyers was it?

Ervin: What do you mean, exactly?

Interviewer: Well, sir, I know the modern judge's breath is so pure a mother could wash her baby with it, but didn't some of the old-time judges take a few drams now and then?

Ervin: Some were accused of "striking a blow for

liberty," to use Vice-President Jack Garner's phrase. And some of the fiery, resolute old judges, like Robert Bruce Pebbles, of Northhampton County, never denied the allegation.

Pebbles must be the only judge in legal history who ever held the entire bar of a county in contempt, simultaneously.

Interviewer: How on earth did that happen?

Ervin: He had the reputation of drinking, and when he got to Lumberton, to hold court in Robeson County, he found all the cases had been postponed. So, he held all the local lawyers in contempt of court. In retaliation, the Robeson bar charged Judge Pebbles with "judicial impropriety," which meant drinking.

Pebbles and some of his friends in Northhampton County tried to dispute the charges with testimonials relative to the judge's drinking. One friend approached Senator Matt Ransom. Now, Ransom, a Confederate brigadier-general, United States Senator, and Ambassador to Mexico, hated Judge Pebbles' guts and Pebbles despised Ransom. Anyway the friend said Judge Pebbles needed help, and Senator Ransom asked, "What's the trouble?" He was told that Pebbles was accused of being drunk in Lumberton.

"That's an obvious lie," Ransom snorted, "There's never been enough whiskey in Robeson County to get old Bob drunk."

Another time Judge Pebbles came here to Morganton to hold court at a time when Burke, our county, was dry, and McDowell County was wet. There was a law making it illegal for anyone to bring as much as a gallon of whiskey from McDowell into Burke.

A man had been arrested for bringing a gallon from

McDowell into Burke, and since he was obviously guilty, his lawyer entered a plea of guilty. Judge Peebles asked for the details and when he heard about the "gallon law," he told the defendant's lawyer: "Change your plea from 'guilty' to 'nolo contendere.' I hereby declare that law unconstitutional. Hell, I brought more than a gallon of whiskey with me when I came here to Burke County to hold court."

Interviewer: You mentioned Senator Matt Ransom a minute ago. Didn't he have the reputation of avoiding his debts?

Ervin: That's what was said. Jonathan Daniels tells the story, in his book *Tar Heels*, I think it is, of the time Ransom owed a large long over-due bill to a Raleigh tailor. The tailor read that Ransom was in Raleigh, and he mentioned to his young, new clerk the large account and his inability to collect it. The clerk, with the impetuosity of youth, spoke up and said he'd bet anything he could collect the debt from Senator Ransom. The boss told him he was most welcome to try, and the clerk said he would see Ransom that very night.

The next morning the clerk came whistling into the shop. The boss, asked, hopefully, "Did you collect any money from Senator Ransom?"

"No, I didn't collect any money," the clerk answered proudly, "But I sold him three new suits."

Interviewer: We were talking, a little while ago, about the days of oratory, when most people in small town and rural society saw the lawyer chiefly in terms of the advocate, the spell-binder. Wasn't there the temptation, at times, certainly, for the lawyer to play up to the audience, as well as to the court, or the jury?

Ervin: Yes, but you have to remember that trying a

case was about the only way the beginning lawyer could "advertize." He couldn't run an ad calling attention to his ability to settle estates, write deeds-of-trust and so on. The real money in a small-town general practice might be in the civil practice, but if a young lawyer sat in his office and waited for so-called money clients to come in, he'd usually have a long, dismal wait.

But if he tried a case well, and if he made a speech to a jury that started people talking, then he'd pick up some clients who needed papers drawn or titles searched.

Interviewer: That's left-handed, but I understand how it was. Undoubtedly, Abraham Lincoln, Zeb Vance and the other wonderful story-tellers were good lawyers, but the heart of their practice was first attracted by their gift with words.

Ervin: You are exactly right. And you have to remember that the young lawyer got the hopeless cases, the ones the established lawyers didn't want. Frequently, in these hopeless trials his only weapons were his wit and words. So, sometimes he was almost in the position of the man Abraham Lincoln described: "He reminds me of the man who murdered both his parents, and then, when sentence was about to be pronounced, begged for mercy on the grounds that he was a helpless orphan."

Nonetheless, the young lawyer was likely to be the chief convert to his own zeal. Usually, he knew his clients in advance, and he could develop a powerful feeling of resentment and indignation if he thought his client had been imposed upon.

For example, people from other states used to come to North Carolina during the season to shoot quail, when the birds were plentiful. Four or five wealthy men from New York state rented a hunting-lodge and hired a dirt

39

farmer to guide them on their daily hunts.

They killed dozens of quails and decided to have a supper at the hunting-lodge, and they asked the guide if he would get such help as he required and prepare the big spread. The farmer asked some relatives to help him, and they spent a whole day preparing the meal. It was only when the out-of-state people sat down to eat that the local people realized they were not guests but menials. It was galling enough that all eating and drinking were done separately, and when the affluent men finished their after-supper brandy and coffee, they dismissed the "cooks" with some loose change.

The "cook" who had been acting as their guide was astonished, and he voiced his vexation and hurt by saying, almost apropos to nothing, "You mean you ain't go have no Bill Bailey? This is all you wanted us for?"

Interviewer: By "Bill Bailey," the man meant the old song, that there was to be no entertainment, no singing, banjo-picking, no dancing?"

Ervin: That's just what he meant, and a big fight broke out, a fist fight, in which the "cooks" mauled the "guests" around. The local men were indicted, and they were guilty, certainly technically, because under our law it constitutes a simple assault just to put your hand on another person in wrath.

The local men employed a young local lawyer, and he was almost livid, sincerely so, at the outrage to his clients. He made the bewildered lament, "You mean there ain't be no Bill Bailey?" the apex of his case and his indignation. As he recounted how his clients had been used and humiliated, he kept intoning to the court, "No Bill Bailey, indeed, Squire." The lawyer was mad enough to fight, genuinely so. He really had blood in his eyes and dynamite on his tongue.

The court had to find the men guilty, but they were assessed a fine of one penny each. So, that was a triumph for impassioned eloquence, righteous indignation.

Interviewer: Yes sir. David Garrick, the great actor, said of George Whitefield, the famous colonial evangelist, "He could make men laugh or cry by pronouncing the word Mesopotamia."

Aside from some of your own speeches, or some your father made, what is the most effective trial speech you ever heard, Senator?

Ervin: I couldn't narrow it to one anymore than I can narrow the best chocolate cake I ever ate to one slice. But for sheer, unadorned simplicity, one of the best I know was told me by an Oxford lawyer when I was a superior court judge and held court in Granville County, and I think the late A.L. Brooks, of Greensboro, told the same story in his memoirs.

A lawyer in Person County, Nathan Lunsford, was or pretended to be, an actheist. He lived about eight miles from Roxboro, the county seat, and each day he rode a bicycle into town. He was one of the first in the county to own a bicycle, and each day he rode across the plantation of a man named Moore, an extremely devout, orthodox Methodist.

Interviewer: When was this?

Ervin: About eighteen ninety-five, I believe.

Interviewer: It was just immediately before this that Dr. James Dunlop, a Scottish physician, made the first rubber bicycle tires when he cut pieces from a garden hose and fashioned tires for his young son's cumbersome iron-wheeled bicycle. So, Lunsford must have bought one

41

of the early rubber-tired bicycles.

Ervin: That's my impression. Anyway, Moore indicted Lunsford for trespass, although it was generally known the real disaffection was Lunsford's professing to be an infidel. He was tried and fined one dollar by a justice of the peace, but he appealed to the Person County Superior Court, and he violated one of the oldest dictums by appearing as his own attorney.

Interviewer: You mean when a man appears as his own attorney he has a damn fool for a client?

Ervin: Yes, that's it. Anyway, practically all of Lunsford's practice was restricted to inferior courts. He was nervous and he was unsure, but he said to the court:

"May it please, Your Honor, I apologize for appearing before this court. I am embarrassed because most of my practice has been confined almost exclusively to appearances before justices of the peace and the probate judge. I did not have the opportunity of acquiring an education, as did Your Honor and the solicitor. I did not begin the practice of law until I was married and had a family of children. The little law I learned was at night by the flame of lightwood knots while my children played around me in the room.

"In his speech the solicitor referred to me as the 'Mogul of Shakerag,' and, thereby reflected on me and the people who live in the ancient and honorable section called Shakerag. If such a tactic is the mark of breeding and education, I rejoice even more in my humble origins.

"Now, Sir, everyone knows the real charge against me is not trespass but religious freedom, the same as was espoused by the great Thomas Jefferson, who came from Monticello and not Shakerag, but the option is the same regardless of birth or residence.

"If I am acquitted, then well may the sheriff say in adjourning the session for the afternoon, 'God save the state and this honorable court.' "

Interviewer: That's terriffic, laid on with a trowel, as Shakespeare said. Lunsford was acquitted, wasn't he?

Ervin: Yes, indeed, and I never heard of a better speech or one put more succinctly.

V

Interviewer: The antithesis of such pristine eloquence, such pared lyricism, must be the story about your man, John Watts, the bricklayer, who thought he was called to preach.

Ervin: John's talents lay in building foundations and not expounding on the gospel, but one day when John was preaching at a rural church, Job Hicks came by, "walking lightly," as they used to say, from the effects of Burke County corn, and Job dragged John from the pulpit. When Job was tried for disturbing religious worship, Judge Robinson said to him, most sternly, "Mr. Hicks, you must have been so intoxicated you really didn't know what you were doing?"

Job replied: "I had several drinks, Your Honor, but I wouldn't want Your Honor to think I was so drunk I could stand by and hear John Watts mumicking up the word of the Lord without doing something about it."

Interviewer: Are they the same two men who had the argument and law suit over the boundary line?

Ervin: Oh, no. Those two were Mark Berry and Uncle Jimmy Mull, both strong Democrats, who lived on adjoining farms. They quarreled and had a big lawsuit. Each was so mad neither spoke for several years. Then one day, about ten years later, when Uncle Jimmy was plowing, Mark walked up to the boundary line and said "Good morning."

Uncle Jimmy bristled, "Mark Berry, what you mean speaking to me after ten years of silence?"

"I came over here to tell you that I'm going to run for sheriff, on the Democratic ticket, and I don't want you or any of your folks voting for me."

Uncle Jimmy kicked a large clod of dirt: "You listen to me, Mark Berry. If you don't want me and my folks to vote for you, then you'll just have to keep your damn name off the Democratic ticket."

Interviewer: The reverse of that story must be the one that's ascribed to Horace Greeley. A New York City Democrat charged that Greeley had said, "All Democrats are saloon-keepers."

Greeley replied, patiently: "I didn't say that. What I said is that all the saloon-keepers I know are Democrats."

Ervin: There's the classic from Granville County, involving Colonel Leonidas Edwards, truly a fire-eating lawyer, and his former slave, Cuffee Mayo. I believe both men served in the legislature, simultaneously, and, on the side, the Republicans gave Cuffee a job cleaning out the state-owned privies in Raleigh. For this work Mayo was paid the then munificent salary of fifteen dollars a week.

Colonel Edwards was making a rousing speech in the House denouncing Republican extravagancies, and he concluded with: "And now, God save the mark, the Republicans have committed the ultimate apostasy by paying Cuffee Mayo fifteen dollars every week to clean out the privies."

Cuffee stood and said calmly, "Marse Lee, mought I ax er question?"

"Of course, Cuffee, ask anything you like."

"Well, en, Marse Lee, how much would you charge to do the same job?"

Interviewer: Colonel Edwards lived in Oxford. His old home is still a handsome place, and his wooden law office, on the large front lawn, is now a small cottage, a home.

Ervin: Yes, and one day when he was walking home to dinner, or lunch, as we call it now, he made an off-hand crack that lawyers the world over have cherished ever since. Sometime before this occasion, a farmer had fallen in with Colonel Edwards on the sidewalk. The farmer had sought some legal help, and Colonel Edwards made some absent-minded reply.

A few months later the farmer fell in on the sidewalk with Edwards as the Colonel was walking to dinner: "Colonel, I did what you told me to do, that time I asked you here on the side-walk, and it worked out mighty bad for me."

Edwards gave the man a contemptuous stare and snorted: "Good God man, don't you know free street advice isn't worth a dried apple dam?"

Interviewer: Many years ago, Senator, a man named R.H. McGuire moved to Oxford from Elizabeth City, from Pasquotank County. McGuire seems to have been a hustler, a shrewd, ambitious man of almost unlimited enterprise. Within a short time of his removal to Oxford he had bought two or three local businesses and he had bought into several others.

He was elected a town commissioner, to his church's

official board, and his family was vital in all of Oxford's social, cultural, dramatic, and artistic affairs. McGuire's name was on office shingles and store-windows all over town, and his family's name was on virtually every tongue, sweetly, except Colonel Edward's, who despised McGuire, denounced him as an arrant interloper.

But McGuire and his family were a tidal wave, and the Colonel and his furies remained isolated and inept until one day he got McGuire into Squire Stovall's magistrate's court, on some minor civil matter. This was the opportunity Colonel Edwards had waited for, and he let out his massive grievances in an hour-long speech, none of which was relevant to the matter at hand.

He talked about world and national problems, and then he got down to local problems. He said Oxford was a nice little place until it was taken over by a "plague of Old Testament proportions and virulence." He went on:

"And, Squire, what is this plague whose inhuman contaminations are infecting our entire community? I can tell you, this new form of black death parades under the devious but nefarious cognomen, R.H. McGuire. I tell you, Squire, no living creature in Oxford can escape the evil implications. Just yesterday afternoon my poor head was reeling blindly from all the endless, craven obeisances uttered about R.H. McGuire. I went into Hall's Drug Store to get something for my miserable head. But could I get waited on? No sir, because everyone was standing around as if in a spell prattling about 'R.H. McGuire, R.H. McGuire.'

"Later I had the same appalling experience when I entered Landis's Store to get a spool of thread for my good wife. And as I started home, after work, stumbling and faltering in pain and in consternation, I entered the

47

barroom of my trusted friend Dick Usry to get a dram for my shattered nerves.

"But could I approach the bar, even get within hailing distance of the affable publican? No, sir, that I could not because the barroom was crowded with garrulous idiots who were mouthing incessant sycophancies about 'R.H. McGuire, R.H. McGuire.'

"Now, Squire, what is this pestilence, who is this plague? In fine, I shall explode the cruel mystery, Sir:

> He comes from down yonder in Pasquotank
> Where the big frogs jump from bank to bank,
> And the little frogs sit in the muck and mire,
> Singing a glad farewell to R.H. McGuire."

Ervin: I guess that "broke up court," rather than causing it to be adjourned. Colonel Edward's extemporaneous poem reminds me of one that someone, maybe Dean Samuel Fox Mordecai, wrote to define drunkenness:

> "Not drunk is he who from the floor
> Can rise again and drink once more;
> But drunk is he who prostrate lies
> Without the will to drink or rise."

And the great Samuel Johnson put it another way: "A man who exposes himself when he is intoxicated has not the art of getting drunk; a sober man who happens occasionally to get drunk readily enough goes into new company, which a man who has been drinking should never do. Such a man is without skill in inebriation."

Interviewer: Courthouse and lawyer literature has

almost disappeared. Of course, there was Earle Stanley Gardner who wrote about Perry Mason the way a short-order cook makes hamburgers for a troop of boy scouts. But the flavorsome, earthy, warts-and-all writers, the local color writers, must be swapping yarns in a melon patch in Beulah Land.

Ervin: Irvin S. Cobb wrote many fine stories about Judge Priest, the salty Kentucky jurist, and a bit more recently I like the stories about "Mr. Tutt," written by Arthur Train, who, I believe, was a lawyer.

Interviewer: Yes sir, and our own poet, John Charles McNeill, was a lawyer, although I don't think he was active in the practice. I am keenly aware that there is much artistic and social objection to any sort of dialect literature today, but, I don't give a damn about that, unless offense is intended. Anyway, Senator, I think one of McNeill's dialect poems, written almost seventy years ago, tells a tremendous story about a vanquished era.

Ervin: I know some of his poetry. How does that one go?

Interviewer:

"I laks to go to coht en see
  Dem lawyers scrappin' all for me.
Dat big jedge, wid de preacher look,
  Readin' in dat air yellow book,
Dem twelve juries listenin' close
  To how I broke ol' Davy's nose,
En all dese people wut you see,
  Deys all in here beca'se a me.

"If I gits out, de gals is mine;
  Day laks a man kin cut a shine.

If I gits in, dey'll feed me free,
  En keep me warm, en let me be
As fat en lazy as I kin,
  —I kinder hopes dey'll putt me in."

Ervin: McNeill was using the mores and idioms of his time, and he certainly didn't intend to demean anyone. His poem is a condensed history of a whole era, a tabloid in verse.

Interviewer: There's a curious bit of minutiae, Senator, but the word "tabloid," in American English, originated to mean such a condensation as you just mentioned. "Tabloid," was a British word that was a registered trade-mark for various patent medicines. Then in American English, it meant anything concise.

Ervin: Then it was finally applied to small sized newspapers that usually printed sensational stories?

Interviewer: That's right, and I think the *Illustrated News*, which began publication in New York City around nineteen hundred and nineteen, was the first newspaper to be called a tabloid.

Ervin: In that poem of McNeill's you quoted, he uses two words, or a phrase and a word, that are rarely ever heard today, — "cut a shine" and "putt." Yesterday the man who could "cut a shine" might also be said to "bore with a big auger" or to "chop with a big ax." He might be outrageous, but people gave him plenty of elbow-room.

I think Mark Twain was way ahead of his time when he talked about the man who acted as if he were waiting for a vacancy to occur in the Trinity. That type is all round now, but there aren't many left among us who can really cut a shine. But such men were doing their

50

own thing long before that phrase was ever known.

And even if it's a mere bagatelle, many educated people said, "Putt 'er there," when they shook hands to bind a deal. Somehow, "putt" still has a good, honest ring to it.

Interviewer: I believe "shine" meant a high mark in school, when it first appeared in the American vernacular, around eighteen fifty. But the thrust of television and various conformities is away from the old, salty colloquialisms, and although you and I and a few "original settlers" retain the ancient regional accent, our local speech and enunciation reflect considerably less of what used to be known as "Tar Heel talk."

A few years ago, the late Bill Polk, of Warrenton and Greensboro, William T. Polk, who wrote that most readable and informative book, *Southern Accent*, said he could tell where a person was from if he heard the person say this sentence: "Mrs. Alexander Cooper's daughter, Mary, had a party last Tuesday."

Ervin: Let's hear what Bill said.

Interviewer: If he says, "Miz Ellexandah Coopuh's dorter Mayry had a pardy lass Chewsday," he is, was, one of us, but if he said, "Misses Alexanderr Coo-per's daughter Merry had a par-tee last Toosday," he comes, or came from somewhere else.

Ervin: As we were saying, the fellow who could "cut a shine" could out-talk, out-eat, out-drink, out-dance, out-hunt, out-smart, out-do just about anyone else in town. He was superlatively indifferent to polls, status-symbols, and other forms of approbation. Local people said if the man who could "cut a shine" ever drowned, they'd look for his body upstream. He was the happy reverse of today's cold calculator who determines

51

the direction of the crowd, gets himself a banner, jumps in front and hollers, "Follow me."

Interviewer: Yesterday such "leaders" were likely to be equated with the man who let himself be called "Honest John."

Ervin: You mean that people hid their silverware and their innocent daughters and kept their gold watches in their pockets when "Honest John" came around?

Interviewer: They certainly did. And as you said, hardly anyone says "putt" today, but it still has a solid ring. But we are talking about that time before national conformity when many educated people said "toe-wards," when underwear was "drawers" and many were made of old flour sacks, when the fellow rhymed "worms" with "Derms" in his newspaper poem, and everyone knew he meant Durham, North Carolina.

Incidentally, Senator, I knew a fellow, a few years back, who could really cut a shine. He could square-dance all night, work hard the next day, and chase fox-hounds the following night. He could do almost anything extremely well, but he didn't talk as if he were a television commercial.

One day he was in a barbershop, and the barber put some rather odoriferous tonic on his hair. A big-mouthed man was in the next chair, and his barber said to him: "You want some tonic like Mr. Parsons just got?"

"Hell naw, you putt that loud-smelling, stinking mess on my hair and when I get home my wife will swear I've been in a whore-house."

Mr. Parsons replied meekly, almost sotto voco: "That doesn't bother me at all because Mrs. Parsons has never been in a whore-house and she doesn't have any idea how one smells."

Ervin: One of the most successful corporate shines was cut by some citizens in ancient Gotham, a village in Nottinghamshire, England. It was announced that King John was seeking a site for a new palace, a summer home. His agents were coming to Gotham, to look it over. The Gothamites, according to legend, didn't want to be burdened with extra, new taxes for the building and maintenance of the palace.

When King John's representatives arrived in Gotham some of the local citizens were trying to drown an eel in a brook. Others had put horses in haymows and men were pulling the haymows. Still others were putting carts atop barns to shield the shingles from the sun, and a large group was trying to make a cage for a cuckoo by joining hands. Obviously King John's agents told him not to build a palace in a place as crazy as Gotham.

Interviewer: Yes sir, and that's why Washington Irving referred to New York City as Gotham, playfully, in his *Salmagundi Papers*, of eighteen hundred and seven.

Senator, this entire little Eastern North Carolina town cut a shine in an impromptu celebration one Saturday night, several years ago. Maybe, I'd better omit the name of the town, or village, but one hot summer night, all the adults in town got drunk. They went to a grocery supply store and got several crates of lemons and several one hundred pound bags of sugar. Then they went to the local ice plant and got a truck load of one hundred pound blocks of ice. They took all this stuff to an old well that survived as a sort of memento.

The ingredients were put into the well and stirred with a bucket, a bucket on a rope, of course, and the lemonade was drawn up by the bucketful. Much of the lemonade was used for chasers but a lot was drunk by children.

Since the children were out so late at night, the man who drove the local fire truck got it out and all the kids took turns riding around the village ringing the bell and blowing the siren. This place still had a town band, of sorts, and the musicians assembled, many in their underwear or nightshirts, to give an informal concert around the well. While the fire truck was running and the band was playing, the north-south train went through town, and the crew and a few passengers, who were awakened, thought they were seeing things.

Ervin: That sounds like something straight from "The Big Rock Candy Mountain."

Interviewer: Senator, we were talking about important and interesting cases a while ago. Now, I know it's impossible to pick one case from so many, from two or three hundred years of legal history, but what do you consider the most "historic" case ever tried in a North Carolina court, and I don't mean, not necessarily, a case that had profound political or social implications?

Ervin: I'll have to think about that for a minute or two. I suppose the one most highly touted, because of recent publicity, was Tom Dula's murder of Laura Foster, in eighteen sixty-six. His name was "Dula," although it appears as "Dooley" in the refurbished song which became so popular. And there was a whole book out about this case, fairly recently.

Interviewer: It's called *The Ballad of Tom Dula*, and the author is John Foster West, one of our mountain boys. And, as you probably know, Glenn Tucker tells about Dula's trials in his prize-winning biography of Zeb Vance, which we have mentioned. Tucker did this because Vance was Dula's colonel during the Civil War and Dula's chief lawyer in the two murder trials.

54

Ervin: After Dula was convicted in Wilkes County, Vance got a change of venue, and the second trial occurred in Iredell County, in Statesville. Dula was convicted again and sentenced to hang. En route from the courthouse to the gallows he rode sitting on the top of his coffin, on a wagon. Then when the sheriff asked if he had any last words to say, old Tom spoke to the crowd for an hour.

Interviewer: Excuse me for butting in Senator, but that's the antithesis of Trampass, one of Owen Wister's characters in *The Virginian*. Some fellows were about to lynch Trampass, but the leader, the man holding the rope, kept gassing away. Finally, Trampass scowled, spat, and asked: "You son-of-a-bitch, are you gonna hang me or talk me to death?"

Ervin: "The court" sustains Trampass. Oliver Wendell Holmes, the poet, not the jurist, said, "Talking is like playing on the harp; there is as much in laying the hands on the strings to stop their vibrations as in twanging them to bring out their music."

Interviewer: Queen Victoria complained that William Gladstone talked to her as if he were addressing a public meeting. Many of us today are so pontifical we do that, just as Tom Dula did to the crowd of on-lookers at his hanging.

Ervin: Yes, that's true enough. When the sheriff was lowering the rope over Dula's head, Tom said to the sheriff, very audibly, "You have such a nice clean rope, I should have washed my neck this morning."

But to get back to your question, if I had to pick one case it would probably be the trial of Frankie Silver, for the murder of her husband, Charlie, back in eighteen thirty-one, and there are a few parallels between this and the Dula matter, which I'll get to.

55

Interviewer: Where did this happen?

Ervin: In our county, Burke, at that time, but the Silvers lived on the Toe River, on the present boundary line between Mitchell and Yancey Counties. These two counties hadn't been formed in eighteen thirty-one and all that region was in Burke County.

Interviewer: Isn't "Toe" supposed to be an abbreviation for "Estatoe?"

Ervin: Yes. According to the accepted story, Estatoe was a princess, the daughter of an Indian chief. She fell in love with a brave from another tribe, apparently from an enemy tribe. They tried to elope, in his canoe, but it swamped and he was drowned. Then Estatoe, completely grief-striken, drowned herself.

Interviewer: My God, that's fantastic, Senator. Those Indians couldn't have known anything about Greek legends, but that's the precise story of Leander and Hero. Leander swam the Helespont, each night, from Abydos, to see Hero, a woman, and when he drowned, accidentally, she threw her body into the sea.

Ervin: And the Indians couldn't have known about *Romeo and Juliet,* even if the Estatoe story must have happened before Shakespeare's time. Maybe, our Indian lore influenced Elizabethan literature. You might even write a paper not only denying that Bacon or Ben Johnson wrote Shakespeare's works but suggesting the bard had his eyes and inspirations turned to these hills.

About the Silver case. Frankie, her real name was Frances, doesn't seem to have revealed her real motive, but she killed her husband, Charlie, sometime during "New Christmas," eighteen thirty-one, probably on December twenty-third.

Interviewer: "New Christmas," Senator?

Ervin: Yes, until about that time in history some people in the remote reaches of our hills, and as far up as the Kentucky mountains, still celebrated "Old Christmas," the fourteen days of Christmas told in song and literature. "Old Christmas" was the last eight days of December and the first six days of January, Epiphany being January sixth.

Interviewer: Christmas day was January six?

Ervin: Yes, that's right.

Interviewer: I think one of the finest mystery stories in the English language is Roy Helton's "Ballad of Old Christmas Morning," a long narrative poem, a marvelous ghost story, with a double-murder, and with the ghost of a slain woman telling the drama. And the late Elizabeth Madox Roberts, the Kentucky novelist and poet, left a fine poem telling how the animals all talked in their stalls on Old Christmas morning.

Ervin: Can you say some of either poem?

Interviewer: Helton's ballad is too long, but here's a little of Elizabeth Madox Roberts' poem:

"If Bethlehem were here today,
Or this were long ago,
There wouldn't be any winter time
Nor any cold or snow.

"I'd run out through the garden gate,
And down along the pasture walk;
And off beside the cattle barns
I'd hear a kind of gentle talk."

And, as you know, "Old Christmas" is still celebrated

each year down at Buxton, on Hatteras. They have "Old Buck" a talking deer, I believe.

Ervin: Correct. For a long time many rural people cherished the lore that all the animals in their barns — the horses, cows, mules, chickens, and pigeons — kneeled and then talked on Old Christmas morning to celebrate Jesus's birthday, just as one of the legends says the animals did in the manger at Bethlehem when Jesus was born.

But to get back to the famous Silver case. It must have been December twenty-second or twenty-third, eighteen thirty-one. Charlie Silver had planned a hunting trip for the next day, and since he'd be gone two or three days, he chopped and split enough fire wood to keep the cabin warm while he was gone.

He seems to have been a pleasant fellow, and it is generally believed that he fell asleep playing with his and Frankie's baby. And as he slept, Frankie killed him with an ax. Then she chopped his body into small pieces and burned it in the fire-place. This required all the wood that Charlie had split, the same amount of fire wood that would usually last several days of cold weather.

Interviewer: This seems to anticipate some sensational murders yet to occur, and some of the overtones remind me of the famous murder mystery, "Two Bottles of Catsup," written a century later. But, I'm baffled, Senator. If Frankie destroyed Charlie's body, how was the crime ever detected?

Ervin: Well, she explained Charlie's absence at Christmas time with the alleged hunting trip. After a few days Frankie told her neighbors something must have happened to Charlie, in the woods, and a searching party of expert trackers went out. All the same, one wily old mountaineer, Jake Cullis, didn't believe Charlie Silver had gone hunting.

He went to the Silver's cabin and he poked around in the fire-place with his staff. He thought the ashes were too greasy, and he found small bones or "pebbles." He raked out one small "pebble" and he put it into a pan of water. When the "pebble" sank to the bottom of the water, grease-bubbles came to the top of the pan.

Several neighbors had collected, and Cullis said "grease bubbles" aloud, but Frankie feigned innocence, almost indifference. However, Cullis and some other men started looking around in the yard, and near the family's well they found a hole that had been filled recently. From the hole Cullis pulled out ashes and some burned metal that neighbors identified as the charred residue of Charlie Silver's belt-buckle.

Some other people pulled out bone fragments and teeth, and finally traces of blood were found on some of the floor planks beside the fire-place. The planks had been scrubbed, rigorously, but the traces of blood were there, and when the planks were pulled out there was a large blotch of blood in the dirt.

Sheriff W.C. Butler was called from Morganton. Frankie denied any knowledge of the crime, and someone seems to have asked Sheriff Butler how such a small woman as Frankie could have carried the body of a man as big as Charlie Silver. Apparently, Frankie, or Frances, weighed around one hundred pounds and her husband about twice that much.

Someone, perhaps the sheriff, reasoned she must have had help from her family. In any event, Sheriff Butler arrested Frankie and her mother and brother, Barbara and Blackston Stewart. The three were jailed here in

Morganton on January nine, eighteen thirty-two, but on January seventeen, in a hearing before two justices of the peace, each was set free on bonds of one hundred pounds, English money, to appear at the March term of court, in Morganton.

Then a grand jury dropped the charges against Barbara and Blackston Stewart, Frankie's mother and brother, but a true bill was returned against Frankie. Frankie's trial seems to have begun on March twenty-nine, and I must give credit here to the enormous research done on this matter by the late Clifton T. Avery, of Morganton.

Old Jake Cullis was one of the chief witnesses for the state, and the teeth, belt buckle and so on were introduced as exhibits. No one knows what evidence Frankie offered; but after the jury had deliberated all night, they returned to the box to request that they be allowed to ask questions of the state's witnesses.

Frankie's attorneys objected, on the ground that these witnesses, kept separated throughout the trial, had been allowed to associate with each other after the case went to the jury.

Judge Donnell, the judge presiding, seems to have thought these objections had some merit, but he reasoned that the jury could not have anticipated need for additional questions, and he over-ruled the motion.

The jury retired, and, apparently on March thirtieth, eighteen thirty-two announced, its verdict. Frankie Silver was guilty of murder; and when Judge Donnell spoke, he announced the first death sentence to be imposed on a woman since North Carolina became a state. She was to remain in jail until the last Friday in July and then to be hanged, on the public gallows here in Morganton.

Frankie's attorneys appealed to the North Carolina

Supreme Court, using the matter of the jury's questioning witnesses after such witnesses had been allowed to associate, but this was denied.

The time consumed in the appeal moved the date of execution to the September term of court. But the judge assigned to hold court, David L. Swain, would become, in December, the youngest governor in North Carolina's history.

Interviewer: This is the same David L. Swain who became President of the University at Chapel Hill?

Ervin: Yes, and he seems to have been busy preparing his new administration and for his inauguration. Whatever the reason, Swain didn't show up in Morganton, and Sheriff Butler declared court adjourned until the spring term of eighteen thirty-three. This meant six months more of life for Frankie Silver.

While she waited in jail, one of her brothers, an expert with a knife, whittled from hard wood a key that fitted the lock on Frankie's cell door. The key was smuggled to her, and she slipped out of jail one night. An uncle of hers, who was waiting outside with a wagon of hay, cut her hair, and dressed her in a man's hat, shirt, pants, and coat.

Burke's new sheriff, John Boone, allegedly a great-nephew of Daniel Boone, organized a posse; and when he over-took the wagon of hay, Frankie was walking behind it, although everyone agreed the hay had been put on the wagon to give her a hiding place.

It's not at all clear that Sheriff Boone recognized Frankie, but he rode his horse close to her and said, "Frances?" She replied, "Thank you, sir, but my name is Tommy." Then her uncle broke in and said, "Yes, her name is Tommy."

"So, *her* name is Tommy?" shouted Boone, as he pulled the hat from Frankie's head. She was brought back to the jail at Morganton and she won another short delay, until July twelfth. She was allowed a few visitors and it is commonly accepted that she confessed her crime to a neighbor from the Toe region, a woman whom she liked.

As the tale goes, Frankie was jealous. She thought Charlie paid too much attention to other women at social affairs. She decided to kill him. He had fallen asleep in front of the fire with their small daughter in his arms. She removed the baby and put her on the bed, and then she hit Charlie a mighty wallop on the neck, with the ax blade. Even so he sprang up and is even credited with screaming, "God bless our child."

He fell to the floor and she applied the coup de grace with a second blow. Then she cut his body up, joint by joint, on the hearth. It took the whole night for her to dispose of the body.

A tremendous crowd turned out on July twelve to see Frankie hanged. Unlike Tom Dula she made no farewell speech. Her father, old Isaiah Stewart, standing in the crowd, yelled, "Die with your secret, Frankie."

Almost as soon as she was dead, some men peddled sheets of paper containing the words of a ballad about Frankie's crime. And many people believed she actually wrote the ballad herself, while she waited in her cell, waited to be hanged.

Interviewer: Well, the ballad is sufficiently clumsy and strained to have been written by a Frankie Silver. Maybe, Frankie did write it.

Ervin: Maybe. Here's a copy of what the peddlers are said to have sold that day:

"One dark and dreary night
I put his body out of sight.
To see his soul and body part,
It strikes with terror to my heart.

"I took his blooming days away,
Left him no time to God to pray,
And if sins fall on his head,
Must I not bear them in his stead?

"The jealous thought that first gave strife
To make me take my husband's life.
For days and months I spent my time
Thinking how to commit this crime.

"His feeble hands fell gently down,
His chattering tongue soon lost its sound.

"My mind on solemn subjects rolls,
My little child, God bless its soul;
All that you are of Adam's race
Let not my faults this child disgrace.

"Farewell, good people, you all now see
What my bad conduct brought on me;
To die of shame and disgrace
Before this world of human race.

"Awful, indeed, to think of death,
In perfect health to lose my breath;
Farewell, my friends, I bid adieu,
Vengeance on me must now pursue.

"Great God, how shall I be forgiven?
Not fit for earth, not fit for Heaven,
But little time to pray to God,
For now I trod that awful road."

Interviewer: "Not fit for earth, not fit for Heaven," reminds me of Kipling's poem about his man, "Tomlinson," who was refused at heaven and hell and returned to his home on Berkley Square until he did something really good or really bad on his own hook.

Anyway, Frankie was hanged for murder, not for bad poetry?

Ervin: I beg your pardon?

Interviewer: Frankie's farewell ballad reminds me of Carl Wanderer, who was hanged for murder in Chicago in the nineteen twenties. Wanderer, a real ham, sang in his cell in the Cook County jail, sang en route to his hanging, and even sang as the rope was being placed around his neck. His piece de resistance was "Dear Old Pal, I Miss You Tonight," and he had just reached this part of the lyrics — "My arms embrace an empty space," — when his neck was broken.

A reporter, who was watching and listening, said, "The son-of-a-bitch ought to have been hanged for his singing voice, if nothing else."

But, Senator, haven't there been attempts to tie Frankie Silver's saga to the old song "Frankie and Johnny," in which Frankie kills Johnny because he two-times her, because "he done her wrong?"

Ervin: I have heard that. I have no opinion, and I understand many variants of "Frankie and Johnny" have existed.

Interviewer: In his *American Songbag,* Carl Sandburg

says "Frankie and Johnny" was born in the eighteen eighties, but Emerson Hough, in his *The Covered Wagon,* fixes the date as eighteen forty, and in this specific connection, I find Hough more reliable. So, if "Frankie and Johnny" appeared in the seamy sections of our cities in eighteen forty, it could have followed a circuitous route from Burke County.

Ervin: That's plausible, certainly, but I really don't know.

Interviewer: Do you know what happened to Frankie's family?

Ervin: According to Clifford Avery, whom I mentioned, and thanked, her mother died shortly afterward from a snake bite; a tree her father was cutting fell on him and smashed his skull; I believe one brother was murdered and another killed in the Civil War; and Blackston, originally indicted with Frankie, was hanged in Kentucky for horse-stealing.

Interviewer: I'd say Charlie's folks, or somebody, really put a first-class curse, an old-fashioned conjure, on Frankie's family.

Ervin: It certainly seems so. It's spooky enough. You know, Francis Bacon said, "Superstition is the reproach of the Diety."

Interviewer: Yes sir, but he was closer to my primitive feelings when he said, "There is a superstition in avoiding superstition."

VI

Interviewer: Excuse me, but a while back one of us mentioned the late Bill Polk. Were you in college with him?

Ervin: Yes, at Carolina and also at the Harvard Law School. As you probably know, he was a lawyer as well as a writer, and he was the mayor of Warrenton, North Carolina, before he became an editorial writer with the *Greensboro Daily News*.

Interviewer: He wrote and told some great stories about Warrenton people.

Ervin: Do you know the story about the two fellows from Warrenton who rode the train to the beach for the first time. They looked at the ocean, and got drunk. One told the other it was time to return to Warrenton. He stuck his pal's return ticket in his hat band and put him on a giant roller-coaster, something the drunk didn't know existed.

Later on someone asked the fellow: "What did you think when that car started hurtling down, zooming down and around so wildly?"

"Well, I turned to George and I told him I thought

that damn railroad bed was a mite rougher than it was when we came up that morning."

Interviewer: Another one of Bill's stories would have social implications superimposed upon it today. He told about the ultra-aristocratic family, in which the father was "worn out" in the Civil War and Junior was born "worn out." The noble wife-mother kept a small-town boarding house; and as she cooked, baked, mended, swept, served, and washed dishes, with the help of one female servant, the old man and Junior sat on the porch, talked of their great days, drank whiskey, and smoked cigars.

But the mother had to change servants each nine months, and after this happened several times the mother said to her son: "Junior, please promise me you'll stay away from the new girl. I'm getting old and good help is hard to come by. I can't keep on making a go of my boarding-house if I have to change help every nine months."

Junior promised faithfully he'd let the new girl alone, but in nine months she had to quit her job to have a baby. The mother accosted Junior: "How could you do such a thing when you promised me on your oath?" Junior sprang from his chair and dropped his highball: "But Ma. It wasn't me, Ma. This time it was Papa."

Senator, Bill wrote a short story called "The Madam Who Saved the State," or something like that. The state senate had a vote coming up on an important educational bill. This was in the early days of this century when Raleigh still had madams and sporting-houses, and the senators who favored the educational bill figured they needed one vote.

If they could obviate one anti-senator, the vote would

end in a tie. Then the lieutenant-governor would cast the tie-breaking vote, affirmatively, and education would go forward. So, two or three pro-senators got this madam to be sure one highly vocal anti-senator wasn't present for the vote.

She entertained him, personally, with charms she never sold but might bestow as an accolade, now and then, and she plied him with her own brandies, and not with the rot-gut sold to her regular trade. Anyway, the man didn't show up for the big vote, and the bill passed, but it was a long time before credit could be given to the madam. Did you ever hear this story, Senator? I mean, is there supposed to be actual substance to Bill's fiction?

Ervin: This is supposed to have happened when I was a boy, and the story was given considerable credence. But if it really happened, as Bill wrote it, the conspirators in the Senate and the madam were bound to silence, and the member who got "kidnapped" certainly couldn't say anything about the ruse. But I suppose it could have happened. Anyway, this legislative deception endured as a sort of open secret for many years.

Interviewer: Unfortunately, the educators and the legislators couldn't express their gratitude with a resolution to the madam, and no editorial writer for a family newspaper could acknowledge the public's indebtedness to the anonymous whore.

Ervin: That's exactly how it was, if it actually happened.

There is another story about this. I understand that a few years later, after the alleged event, someone who was privy to the shenanigans, saw a brand-new schoolhouse and gave an on-the-spot twist to a line Shakespeare has in *Othello*: "This is the fruit of whoring."

Interviewer: And to be equally as facetious, Senator, one is almost forced to lament, "They just don't make whores like that anymore."

We've done a good deal of spontaneous quoting today, and I wonder if you are aware some of your recent quotes in speeches and interviews have whetted much interest in that ancient literary-form, the epitaph?

Ervin: No, I didn't know that, but if it's happened, I'm glad.

Interviewer: How does the one go that you ascribe to the late John Rankin, Congressman from Mississippi?

Ervin: John told the story about this man whose hobby was browzing around old cemeteries to read the epitaphs on gravestones. This man even carried a piece of chalk with him so he could bring out faded inscriptions, and one day he came across this inscription:

"Pause thou, stranger, passing by,
As you are now, so once was I.
As I am now, you soon will be.
Prepare for death and follow me."

John Rankin's man pulled out his piece of chalk and added this postscript:

"To follow you, I'll not consent,
Until I find which way you went."

Interviewer: I believe epitaphs originated with the Egyptians.

Ervin: That's my impression. The Greeks often had long, flowery epitaphs, but the Romans had shorter, more succinct, inscriptions on their gravestones.

Interviewer: That's right, sir, and because most of the Roman graves were alongside the highway, many tombstones had the injunction, "Sta, Viator," or "Stop, traveler."

Ervin: And ever since their origin, epitaphs have run a wide gamut, from the stately to the frivolous, even the ribald. But I think Samuel Johnson put the whole business of such inscriptions in proper focus when he said, "In lapidary inscriptions a man is not bound upon oath." Johnson went on to say that some allowance must be made "for some degree of exaggerated praise."

Interviewer: And our own caustic Ambrose Bierce defined an epitaph: "An inscription on a tomb showing that virtues acquired by death have retroactive effect."

Ervin: Some have been pretty fulsome, but I like the mass epitaph of the three hundred young Spartans, under Leonidas, who died at the pass of Thermopylae, around 480 B.C.: "Stranger, tell the Lacedaemonians that we lie here, obedient to their commands."

Interviewer: That's certainly one of the most eloquent and touching, and I like the one that Sir Christopher Wren's son wrote on his tomb in St. Paul's Cathedral: "Si momumentum requiris circumspice," or "If you would see this monument, look about you."

Ervin: Yes, Sir Christopher Wren built St. Paul's Cathedral. And someone suggested this epitaph for Copernicus: "Sta, Sol, ne moveare," or "Stand, oh, Sun, move not."

Interviewer: Dorothy Parker suggested, "Excuse my dust," for her own epitaph, and I like the one Benjamin Franklin wrote for his gravestone, even if it is a bit ornate by today's standards:

"The body of
Benjamin Franklin, printer,
(Like the cover of an old book,
Its contents worn out,
And stript of its lettering and gilding)
Lies here, food for worms!
Yet the work itself shall not be lost,
For it will, as he believed, appear once more
In a new
And more beautiful edition,
Corrected and amended
By its Author."

Ervin: The essence of this one takes many forms, I'm
told, but I'm sure the implications are applicable to most
of us:

"Here lie I, Martin Elgingrodde:
Hae mercy o' my soul, Lord God;
As I wad do, were I lord God
And ye were Martin Elgingrodde."

Victor Hugo said of Napoleon: "God was bored with
him," and in *Hamlet*, Shakespeare really dusted off
Julius Caesar:

"Imperious Caesar, dead and turn'd to clay,
Might stop a hole to keep the wind away."

Ervin: Some lines supposed to be on the stone of one
Mike O'Day, a hard-headed motorist, are grimly pertinent
at the moment.
Interviewer: Say the lines, please.

Ervin:

"Here lies the body of Mike O'Day
Who died maintaining his right of way,
His right was clear, his will was strong,
But he's just as dead as if he'd been wrong."

Interviewer: Right on, Senator. Apparently, John Wilmot, the Earl of Rochester, wrote this epitaph for Charles II while the king was still living:

"Here lies our Sovereign Lord, the King,
Whose word no man relies on.
He never said a foolish thing
And never did a wise one."

Ervin: And Alexander Pope paid his respects to Lord Coningsby in much the same spirit:

"Here lies Lord Coningsby-be civil!
The rest God knows-perhaps the Devil."

Interviewer: Some wag wrote these lines when Frederick, Prince of Wales, died in 1751:

"Here lies Fred,
Who was alive and is dead;
Had it been his father,
I had much rather.
Had it been his brother,
Still better than the other;
Had it been his sister,
No one would have missed her;

Had it been the whole generation,
All the better for the nation;
But since 'tis only Fred,
That was alive and is dead,
Why, there's no more to be said."

Ervin: That could have been written by an American, an irate colonist. While some of our place names — New Hanover, Charlotte, and Mecklenburg — commemorate the family names, many of our ancestors took an exceedingly dim view of the whole tribe of Hanover.

Interviewer: I understand Oliver Cromwell and John Hampden had papers for the Massachusetts Bay Colony, were actually aboard ship, when a royal proclamation was served, one that forbade sea captains from having "political passengers."

Ervin: Yes, Cromwell stayed and Charles' proclamation cost him his head, but it is intriguing to speculate on what the history of England would be if Cromwell had come to Massachusetts; and it's even more interesting to speculate on what Cromwell's presence in this county would have done.

Interviewer: Senator, have you seen the movie about "Judge" Roy Bean, the man who called himself "the law west of the Pecos?"

Ervin: No, but I know some of the wild stories about the so-called judge. Once when he was supposed to be holding an inquest relative to a homicide, the body of the deceased was brought into Bean's court. Bean fined the corpse forty-two dollars and twenty-eight cents for carrying a concealed weapon.

Interviewer: That was the precise amount of money the deceased had in his jeans?

Ervin: To the penny, and the weapon was concealed because the dead man was lying face-down, with his holster under his belly.

Interviewer: Somehow, Bean's finding the corpse reminds me of an old cartoon in the *New Yorker* magazine. This couple walks into a police station, carrying a rumble-seat, and they say to the desk-sergeant, "We want to report a stolen car."

Ervin: Yeah, but not many today may know what a rumble-seat is or was.

Interviewer: But even in frontier society, judges such as Roy Bean were phenomena, weren't they, Senator?

Ervin: Yes, indeed. They were sporadic and they were temporary aberrations produced by extremely necessitous times. You have to remember the manner in which the frontier was settled. The late Frederick Jackson Turner, in his book, *The Significance of the Frontier in American History*, once thought to be a classic, tells how three distinct classes of people, like waves of the ocean, rolled across the nation's frontiers. First came the pioneer who built a crude cabin and lived off the land. He brought with him a few animals, and he gathered a few other families on his "range." He lived rent-free, and when he pushed on for the "tall timber," he sold his cabin and land to immigrants who put glass windows and curtains in the cabins, built a grist-mill, a schoolhouse, a courthouse, and so forth.

The third wave was composed of men of capital. When the men of capital and business enterprise came, the village becomes a town, and the town becomes a city.

Until the second wave of immigrants came you find examples of crudest justice, even men such as Roy Bean, if he actually existed, but this harsh legal expediency

74

existed only when there was a condition of extreme transition.

Interviewer: Didn't the same thing happen occasionally in the original colonies, especially in the back-country?

Ervin: Yes, and that is how we get the phrase, "kick-the-bucket," meaning to die. In the days in the back-country, before the courts were really organized, a sheriff would apprehend a horse-thief, assemble a so-called jury, and then try and convict the man, all within a few minutes. The sheriff would throw a rope over a stout limb, tie the rope around the man's neck, and place the man on a regular bucket. Then the sheriff would kick the bucket and let the man swing, die.

Interviewer: I think it was Frederick Jackson Turner, whom you just quoted, who pointed out how European life came to this untamed continent to be developed and modified by a strange, new American environment. The frontier was the quickest agency in Americanization. The colonist was a European in dress, customs, and thought, but he was mastered very quickly by his new environment.

Ervin: Yes, that's it, almost precisely. When the Atlantic coast was the frontier, it was still European, in thought and customs, but as the frontier moved to the west, it became more and more American, more and more of the natural environment.

Interviewer: Did you ever know, or know of, an actual judge comparable to Roy Bean?

(Ervin does not answer immediately for laughing.)

Ervin: We had one here in North Carolina. I never saw him, but I heard so much about him I think I knew him intimately. This was Judge Samuel Watts, a product of the extreme transition of carpetbag rule. Watts's lack of judicial temperament was matched by his massive dishevelment, and Josiah Turner, editor of the Raleigh *Sentinel*, who had a diabolical genius for giving his enemies lasting nicknames, dubbed him "Greasy Sam" Watts.

Interviewer: You mean Turner referred to the judge in his newspaper as "Greasy Sam?"

Ervin: Oh, Lord, yes, and frequently without any elucidation, to make it even more effective. Turner would merely write: "Last week Greasy Sam Watts held court in Hillsborough."

Interviewer: Watts wasn't remotely qualified to be a judge?

Ervin: Not in a thousand years. His chief talent was drawing caricatures and this was his abiding interest. He sat on the bench, oblivious to what was going on in his court, and drew caricatures of the various lawyers, jurors, witnesses, and court officials.

Now, back before we had any public-supported high schools, some of our private preparatory schools, such as the famous ones operated by Bingham and Horner, would declare a holiday on "Chewsday of Coat Week" so that the students could attend the day's session of court.

On one such Tuesday, "Greasy Sam" had gathered fifteen or twenty boys, students, around the bench, and the boys looked over his shoulder as he sketched his caricatures. "Greasy Sam's" art lay in distortion. He would make the tall, thin man three feet high and wide, and vice versa. He would make one subject all ears and another all Adam's apple.

As the boys watched he is supposed to have made a lawyer, arguing to the jury, a facsimile of a braying billy-goat. The boys laughed, and "Greasy Sam" laughed so heartily at his handiwork he broke his glasses and had to adjourn court sine die, for the term.

Interviewer: Was Watts aware of the general feeling about him? Did this bother him?

Ervin: He never seemed to have let asperities bother him, but he had an unusual exchange with Colonel Leonidas Edwards, whom we've talked about.

Interviewer: What happened?

Ervin: "Greasy Sam" was holding court in Oxford, and he had adjourned court, sine die, but he remained on the bench for a while, writing something, or, more likely, finishing off some caricatures. Colonel Edwards approached the bench and asked sweetly, quietly, almost reverently: "Your Honor, has court adjourned?"

Watts mumbled "Yes" without looking up, and Edwards asked, in the same soft, deferential tone, "Is Your Honor sure court has adjourned?" Watts said he was sure, and then Edwards asked if court had been adjourned sine die. At this, "Greasy Sam" put down his art equipment and said, "Yes, Mr. Edwards, why?"

Edwards roared out: "Because, in that event, may God Almighty never afflict this court again with the likes of such a blatherskite and ignoramus as you."

Interviewer: What did Watts do?

Ervin: He called the sheriff, had him convene court, and he fined Colonel Edwards fifty dollars for contempt, a lot of money back then. Edwards didn't have fifty dollars on him, but people in and around the courthouse made up the balance hurriedly. He counted the bills, handed them over to Judge Watts, and bellowed out: "My friends and I want you to know that fifty dollars doesn't even begin to start to commence to express the contempt we hold for you and your damned court."

Interviewer: Did anybody ever write up "Greasy Sam?"

Ervin: Not to my knowledge, not per se; but since you are a fan of Thomas Wolfe, you probably know he has a character in *The Hills Beyond,* one of his posthumous books, whom he calls Greasy Ray. This minor character must be a combination of fact and lore. Obviously, Wolfe had heard about "Greasy Sam," and he seems to have applied the unsavory nickname to Judge Bis Wray, whom he fictionalizes as "Greasy Ray."

Interviewer: Judge Greasy Ray is the man who gets lost going to Harrington to hold his first court?

Ervin: That's the story.

Interviewer: Did it really happen?   I mean the way Thomas Wolfe told it in his story?

Ervin: Wolfe's fiction is based on a story that was well established when I started the practice of law. Bis Wray, of Burnsville, Yancey County, was appointed a Superior Court Judge, and his first court was at Manteo, on the other side of the state.

Interviewer: Excuse me, but Wolfe calls Manteo "Harrington?"

Ervin: That's right. In Wolfe's story the judge is thrilled at the opportunity to see so much of the world. He sets out for Harrington, but he has to change trains and railroad lines several times. The last portion of the trip has to be made by ferry-boat. The judge goes to sleep on the ferry, wakes up at the dock, takes a hack to the nearest hotel, and demands that the manager call the sheriff.

The astounded sheriff comes to the judge's room and asks what he wants. The judge tells him: "I am Judge

Ray and I am here in Harrington to hold court. So, let's open it."

"Good God, man, this ain't Harrington, this is Baltimore."

Interviewer: In actuality, in those days, one would have taken the ferry from Elizabeth City across to Roanoke Island. So, if one took the wrong ferry, he could end up in Baltimore?

Ervin: That's possible, certainly, especially depending upon one's condition when one reached Elizabeth City.

Interviewer: *Look Homeward, Angel,* which caused all the furor in Asheville, Wolfe's home-town, came out in nineteen twenty-nine, and he didn't return home again until nineteen thirty-seven, the year before his death. He came back through Bristol, Tennessee-Virginia, and into Burnsville, where some of his mother's people lived; and he must have hit upon Judge Wray's alleged misadventure at that time. Then he remembered "Greasy Sam" Watts, dropped the "W" from "Wray," and came up with Greasy Ray.

Ervin: That's about the way it must have happened.

Interviewer: In two or three places in *The Hills Beyond* he tells about a murder and the subsequent trial. Now, one of the things that really interests me is that the actual defendant was Judge Bis Wray's son.

I knew the defendant, and the man he killed, superficially anyway, and it always interested me that Wolfe transported their personalities, mannerisms, and family backgrounds when he wrote about the homicide which he witnessed.

Ervin: What Wolfe did reminds me of this true story that happened in Morganton, one that involved marriages between two widows and two widowers. This lady who was a Presbyterian married a man who was a Methodist and he joined her church. This man who was Presbyterian married a lady who was a Methodist, and he joined her church.

Our sheriff, a most caustic commentator, was watching the first Sunday the two men went to their new churches. He shook his head, spat, and said: "This is an even-swap in which both sides got stuck."

Interviewer: Yes sir, and similar to the one I believe was told about Henri Watterson. Watterson was supposed to speak on "Money," but the man who introduced him got mixed up and said Watterson would speak on "Morals." When the introducer discovered his error, he told the audience: "Well, it really doesn't make any difference because our speaker (Watterson) doesn't have any more morals than he has money."

Ervin: I should add in passing that "Greasy Sam" Watts performed one notable service for our system of justice. When he was on the bench, judges might serve the same court for six months, even a year. But no county wanted to get stuck with "Greasy Sam." So, the bar association arranged the present system whereby judges are rotated, the same as Methodist preachers, and no county gets blessed, or stuck, with the same jurist more than the allotted period.

Interviewer: How do you suppose such a man ever qualified to practice law?

Ervin: "Qualify?" That reminds me of the time the illiterate man came to the office of a fiesty old mountain clerk-of-the-court. The clerk snarled: "What are you doing in my office, Tom Smith?"

"I come here to qualify fer jestice of the peace."

"Qualify, hell. It would take God Almighty to qualify

you, but hold up your damn hand and I'll swear you in."

Anyway, your asking me how "Greasy Sam" qualified to practice law reminds me of the story from the old days when a boy from away back in the sticks appeared before a judge and a small committee of lawyers to take his bar examination.

The boy's name was Josh, and the judge said to him: "Josh, before we can qualify you to follow our jealous mistress, we must touch upon your legal training. And we assume you have grounded yourself in the great teachings of Blackstone."

"What'd you say his name was Jedge?"

"Blackstone, Sir William Blackstone, the father of the English common law."

"Did he live around?"

"Unfortunately, he didn't, but, perhaps, you have specialized in Coke instead of Blackstone?"

"No sir, I ain't been out with him none to speak of."

"Well, then, Josh, we don't want to sound unduly inquisitive; but since we have a solemn duty to perform, might we ask if you have familiarized yourself with the Constitution of the United States and the Constitution of the great commonwealth of North Carolina?"

"To be honest, I ain't messed with them much yet."

"Well, Josh, my son, we ask your pardon if you think we pry too deeply into your intimate affairs, and we want to assure you that we are not moved by morbid curiosity alone; but would you tell us just what studying you have done in preparation for this exalted goal of yours?"

"Well, sir, and suzz, there's a book in Jedge Bynam's office called *Volume Twenty-Three, Revised Statutes of*

North Carolina, that I projecked around with a right smart."

"God Almighty, Josh, the next session of the legislature is likely to repeal every damn thing you know."

Interviewer: A minute ago you mentioned the fiesty clerk-of-the-court. I heard of one in the old days who drank so much whiskey people were afraid to light cigarettes close to him. One day the town's blind man knocked this clerk down on the street twice, twice in the same day, because the blind man thought the clerk was the swinging door to the saloon.

This clerk couldn't keep his various books intact. Lawyers were always walking off with his books and the clerk never had them when he needed them. So he agreed to pay a young, hungry lawyer, a shyster, I fear, two bits for each book he returned.

For a while the lawyer would make the rounds of other lawyers' offices and bring back a book and collect his twenty-five cents. Then, seeing a real bonanza, the hungry lawyer started taking books from the clerk's office to his own office. By the first of the month, when this shyster had to pay his board and room, he'd be seen pushing a wheelbarrow filled with books to the drunk clerk's office.

Ervin: Now, Disraeli never heard of this arrangement, but he might have been thinking of it when he wrote: "Collections of books are subject to certain accidents, one not less common is that of borrowers, to say nothing of the purloiners."

Interviewer: This isn't apropos, but what did Job mean when he said, "Oh, that mine adversary had written a book?"

Ervin: The King James version, which you just quoted, is a bit misleading to the modern reader, but the *Revised Standard Version* makes it clearer. What Job is really saying is that he wishes God had written out a bill of specific charges against him, a formal indictment. Job is saying that he can't refute any charges and prove his innocence unless he knows what he is accused of doing, of having done.

Interviewer: Thank you very much. Many of the critics who pretend to know everything, read everything, remind me of Jonathan Swift's deathless crack: "There are men who pretend to understand a book by scouting through the index, as if a traveler should go about to describe a palace when he had seen nothing but the privy."

Forgive me, but there is a follow-up to the story of the clerk's books. The shyster was approached by a poor, ignorant woman whose son was in jail. She asked how much he'd charge to get her boy out of jail and he said he could do it for ten dollars, cash money.

She asked if he was certain he could get her boy out of jail and he assured her he could. She gave him the ten dollars and he had the boy subpoenaed as a witness in a case being tried in the Superior Court.

Ervin: You mean a case about which the poor boy knew absolutely nothing?

Interviewer: Yes sir. The Sheriff brought the boy over from the jail and carried him back within a matter of minutes when the court learned the boy knew nothing of the matter at hand. The irate mother grabbed the shyster by his lapels: "You lied to me, you scoundrel, you. You said you could get my boy out of jail."

"That's what I said, Madam, and that's what I did. I

never guaranteed to keep him out of jail."

The lawyer was, as people used to say, as Josephus Daniels liked to put it, a son-of-a-bitch, Net.

Ervin: Precisely. Adding "Net" doubled him, and in spades.

Interviewer: Today you never hear it said that a man is so low-down and common he'd need a step-ladder to climb up to a snake's belly.

Ervin: Nor anything about the man who is so sorry anybody could take a Barlow knife and carve a better specimen of humanity out of a shingle.

Interviewer: We don't use the old phrase very often, but the fellow is still around who thinks it meet and proper to send his mother a congratulatory telegram on the occasion of his own birthday.

VII

Interviewer: There used to be the story, and apparently it wasn't apocryphal, about the man from the Piedmont who had business in a county seat town in the mountains. The county seat town was only a village, and the visitor from the Piedmont was astounded to see all the sidewalks crowded with people, as folks were lined up waiting to get in the courthouse.

The visitor saw one strange-looking man more or less detached from the crowd. The fellow was dressed in a bright, checked suit, a red tie, a pink shirt, and spats. The visitor asked, "What are all these people doing? What on earth is going on?"

"They are going into the courthouse for the trial."

"What kind of trial? Murder?"

"No, it is a buggering case."

"Well, aren't you going?"

"Absolutely. I am the gentleman who was buggered."

To bring in a gentleman of the cloth may seem impertinent at this precise juncture; but I want to ask you, Senator, before I forget it, had the Reverend Doctor J.

William Jones passed on before your undergraduate days at Chapel Hill? I ask because I ran across a Civil War article of his in an encyclopedia a couple of days ago.

Ervin: No, but the place was still alive with his prayers, or lectures, to the Lord.

Interviewer: As I understand it, Jones was a Confederate chaplain who made Robert E. Lee a form of active worship. After the war he became the Baptist minister at Lexington, Virginia, solely to be near General Lee, an Episcopalian, then President of Washington College, now Washington and Lee University. Then after Lee's death and the gradual demise of the Confederate veterans in and around Lexington, Virginia, he moved to Chapel Hill and became chaplain of the University of North Carolina.

Ervin: That's right, and he did all of the official praying. That splendid writer, Phillips Russell, of the class of nineteen hundred four, now a hale and virile eighty-nine, gives this verbatim prayer that Jones delivered to close a mighty convocation at Chapel Hill: "Lord we acknowledge Thee as the all-wise author of every good and perfect gift. We recognize Thy presence and wisdom as much in the terror of lightning as we recognize Thy presence and wisdom in the healing shower. We acknowledge Thou had a divine plan when Thou made the rattle-snake, as well as the song bird, and this was without help from Charles Darwin. But we believe Thou will admit the grave mistake in giving the decision to the wrong side in eighteen hundred and sixty-five. But in spite of this and the tragic confusion of divine intentions at Chancellorsville, and the third day at Gettysburg, Thou art eternal and we lean our frailties on Thy everlasting arms."

Interviewer: The "tragic confusion at Chancellorsville" would be shooting of Stonewall Jackson by his own men?"

Ervin: Yes.

Interviewer: Gamaliel Bradford, the broker who turned historian and wrote such superlative portraits, was fascinated by Jones. In his extraordinarily human book about Robert E. Lee, Bradford quotes Jones a little, where Jones had written, "Speaking only comparatively, there is no doubt that General Lee is the greatest military genius in history." Bradford adds this chuckle: "There's no telling what the reverend gentleman would have said if he hadn't been speaking 'only comparatively.'"

Ervin: Frank Stringfellow, the Confederate spy, and about as audacious and ferocious as anyone who ever lived, became a crusading Episcopal minister after the war. When Grant came down from Washington to take command of the army opposing Lee, Stringfellow blew up his train, but Grant had waited for a second train.

Interviewer: I understand Stringfellow weighed only about a hundred pounds and that he was as pretty as a girl.

Ervin: Yes, and when he was in college, at Virginia, I believe, he played Juliet and other women's roles in undergraduate dramas. There weren't any co-eds to play these parts.

Interviewer: About Stringfellow's size. This is told for the truth: Some Union intelligence people flushed Stringfellow in Winchester, Virginia. Stringfellow started running, somewhat wildly, and, without any plan, he turned down an alley. He came to a kitchen door and he ran inside. A girl, someone he knew, was sitting there in a chair, and wearing a voluminous, floor-length dress, a hoop-skirt, I suppose. Anyway, she surmised the problem immediately. She yanked up her skirts, cried, "Here, Frank," and he crawled under. She straightened out her skirts and Stringfellow's pursuers almost tore the house down looking for him.

Ervin: Some of those really ferocious Confederates were just as ferocious when they took after Satan after the war.

Interviewer: Maybe, they thought one was a continuation of the other. They merely swapped Yankees for the devil.

Ervin: Probably so. I believe it was Stringfellow who came to town to conduct a revival. He asked that all the saloons be closed while he preached each day, but one bar-keeper wouldn't close. In his main prayer, Stringfellow told the Lord about local conditions, including the uncooperative saloon-keeper. That same night the saloon-keeper had a stroke; thereafter there was no reluctance to shut down the bars while Stringfellow preached.

Interviewer: May ten, Confederate Memorial Day, used to be a terrific event.

Ervin: Until around nineteen fifteen it was the biggest of all local celebrations in North Carolina. Every town had picnics, barbecues, ball games, endless oratory, and all of the various festivities were topped by a parade of the Confederate veterans. The bands played "Dixie" and the way the old soldiers rattled their canes and roared the Rebel Yell was enough to make Mount Mitchell topple.

Interviewer: Didn't special excursion trains run to many places just for May ten?

Ervin: Yes, they certainly did, and that reminds me of an old mountaineer, a real "Doubting Thomas," who rode into Morganton to see his first locomotive, his first train. The locomotive and cars, carrying dignitaries and bands and decked with bunting, stood on the tracks at the station. This old fellow looked at it and said, "Aye, God, they'll never get her started." Then when the train started and took off in the direction of Marion, he shook his head and exclaimed, "Aye, God, they'll never get her stopped."

Interviewer: That reminds me of one of the first small, passenger planes I ever saw. There seemed to be some engine trouble. The plane was flying dangerously low, and it bounced up and down. This black friend of mine was standing beside me looking at this erratic passenger plane, and he said: "Well, if that's how they're going to be, they won't have to bother putting in any goddam Jim Crow section."

And I think this story about May ten is true: A daily sent a reporter to cover some super-duper May ten celebration in a small town. The editor cautioned the reporter about the habitual cliches. The editor explained: "For God's sake don't write something as trite as 'the Gray lines are thinner' or 'the heads are grayer and thinner."

Ervin: What originality did your man come up with?

Interviewer: His lead was, "My God, didn't they sweat that corn whiskey, and, good God, didn't their corns hurt."

But in line with the unusual praying of Jones and Stringfellow, what's that story about Carlton Giles?

Ervin: CALTON, Calton Giles and Billy Hallyburton were inseparable friends, tomb-stone buddies. They hunted and fished together, and they were both staunch Democrats. One time they attended a Methodist revival, and they were so moved by the spirit they professed religion and joined the Methodist church. They agreed that each day for the rest of their lives they would get down on their knees and pray for each other.

Then in eighteen ninety-six Billy Hallyburton attended a Populist rally when that movement was sweeping North Carolina. Billy responded to the Populist rousements and he joined the party, forthwith. This happened in the afternoon, and at two a.m. the following morning, Billy was awakened by a loud knocking at his door, and Billy asked who was knocking at such an unearthly hour.

"Brother Billy, it's Calton Giles. As I was about to go to bed tonight, I heard a foul slander on you, and I took off my nightgown and hitched up my horse to hear you deny the slander with your own Christian lips."

"What foul slander did you hear, Calton?"

"I heard you had left the Democrats and joined the Populists."

Uncle Billy told him: "That's no slander, Calton, that's the truth."

Calton replied: "You remember when we were boys and promised to pray for each other everyday so long as we lived? Well, every night since then I have gotten down on my knees and prayed for you. But, Brother Billy, from now on you can do your own goddam praying."

Interviewer: What was it Dr. Hale, the Chaplain of the Senate, said?

Ervin: Someone asked Hale: "Doctor, when you pray, as Chaplain of the Senate, do you think of the many tragic problems of the nation and then pray that the

90

Almighty will give these Senators the wisdom to deal with these problems?"

Hale answered: "No, I don't look at the country and pray for the Senators. I look at the Senators and pray for the country."

Interviewer: That's the same man, Edward Everett Hale, who wrote "The Man Without a Country?"

Ervin: Yes. He was a Congregationalist minister and a most prolific writer. He published "The Man Without A Country" in the *Atlantic Monthly* in eighteen sixty-three, anonymously. He wrote many books, including a most readable one about Benjamin Franklin's stay in Paris, and in his old age he was Chaplain of the Senate, from about nineteen hundred to nineteen six.

Interviewer: I suspect Philip Nolan, the tragic hero of "The Man Without a Country" is better known than Hale, the man who created the character.

Ervin: I think you are about right. Raffles, the gentlemanly safe-cracker, was better known than E.W. Hornung, his creator, and Jeeves is as well known as P.G. Wodehouse, I should think.

Interviewer: True enough, and everyone used to sing "Will You Love Me In September, As You Do In May," but few ever knew the lyrics were written by Jimmy Walker, New York's flamboyant mayor.

Ervin: Until recently virtually everyone was familiar with the fiery injunction, "You Kansas farmers would be better to stop raising corn and start raising hell," but few knew the words were spoken by a woman, Mary Elizabeth Lease.

Interviewer: She was called "the Kansas Pythoness," wasn't she?

Ervin: She's the one. As I said, her name was Mary

Elizabeth, but some newspaper had her middle name as "Ellen," erroneously, but this produced a national play on words, "Mary Yellin'," and Mrs. Lease was "Mary Yellin' " to America's embattled farmers of the eighteen nineties.

Interviewer: She was one of the original Women's Libbers, wasn't she, Senator?

Ervin: Absolutely. She espoused full women's rights, along with postal savings banks, government operation of utilities, agrarian reforms, rural free delivery of mail, and stricter government control of banks. As a matter of fact, she was drafted as a candidate for governor of Kansas back about eighteen ninety-six, long before women got the vote. The Populists drafted her while she was on a national lecture tour. She spoke two or three times in North Carolina, for the Populists, and Billy Hallyburton went to hear her, I'm sure.

Interviewer: But not Calton Giles?

Ervin: Not on your tintype. As a matter of fact "Mary Yellin' " lived until about nineteen thirty-three, I'm sure she was as least eighty, but she had been forgotten by all the new political reformers. Many of her ideas, the suggestions made by the Populists, became a part of F.D.R.'s New Deal, under slightly different names, in new rainment; but even though she lived, "Mary Yellin' " was as defunct and passe as the battleship *Maine*.

Interviewer: Housman writes about the same thing in his poem "To An Athlete Dying Young." The athlete, a runner, in Housman's poem dies while his triumph is fresh. Housman says:

"Smart lad to slip betimes away
From fields where glory does not stay,
And early though the laurel grows
It withers quicker than the rose."

Then he drives his nail down in another stanza:

"Now you will not swell the rout
Of lads that wore their honors out,
Runners whom renown outran
And the name died before the man."

Ervin: That's somewhat similar to Oliver Wendell Holmes', "And if I should live to be/The last leaf upon the tree/In the spring,/Let them smile, as I do now,/At the old forsaken bough/Where I cling." And I understand Holmes' actual model was Major Thomas Melville, Herman Melville's grandfather, a Revolutionary War veteran who was living in eighteen thirty-two, when Holmes wrote the poem, and still wearing the old-fashioned knee-britches and three-cornered hat which were popular during George Washington's time.

Interviewer: I've always liked that poem, and I don't give a damn what the self-winding sophist says about it. As you know, Holmes was born in eighteen nine and lived until eighteen ninety-four, and near the end of his life he said he lasted long enough to serve as an illustration for his own poem.

Ervin: Eighteen nine was some year. As I recall Holmes, Tennyson, Edgar Allen Poe, Abraham Lincoln, Charles Darwin and perhaps other notables, were all born that same year. I suppose, though, that Lincoln is the only one who qualifies as a "self-made man," in the old sense.

Interviewer: I imagine so. I knew a lawyer, who attained considerable eminence, who bragged incessantly of his triumph over the lack of opportunities and the parlous conditions of his youth. When he was among college graduates, especially lawyers, he never lost an opportunity to say, "I am not a degree man. I am a self-made man." He meant he didn't have a chance to attend undergraduate school. He'd go on to explain how he had obtained all of his formal education in one year in law school. Then he'd add, "I am not a degree-man, I am a self-made man."

Another lawyer became threadbare hearing "I am not a degree-man. I am a self-made man." So, when the eminent lawyer had made his habitual spiel, the other lawyer nodded and said: "Yes, damn it, we all know you are a self-made man and are goddam proud of your creator."

Ervin: Yes. This is a true story, too. This man, a fine man, who was born out of wedlock, was talking to a highly successful, crook, an unconvicted crook, and a man who exuded the fraudulent piety of Elmer Gantry. The professional Christian became irritated at the other man, lost his composure, and shouted, "You damn bastard."

The fellow born out of wedlock replied: "In my case, that's purely an accident of birth. In your case that's a fact of life you've worked hard to solidify across the past forty years."

VIII

Interviewer: That's somewhat similar to the time Speaker of the House Thomas Reed had to listen to the pompous Congressman who kept beating his breast and saying "I'd rather be right than President." Reed answered, calmly: "The gentleman need have no apprehensions. The chances of his ever being either are entirely remote."

Ervin: Of course, Henry Clay was the first to say he'd rather be right than President, and John Randolph," Randolph of Roanoke," may have said substantially the same thing Thomas Reed said later on. But it was about Edward Livingston that Randolph made his really deathless denunciation, or slander: "He is a man of splendid abilities, but utterly corrupt. He shines and stinks like rotten mackerel by moonlight."

Interviewer: Ironically, that savage denunciation gave Livingston a type of left-handed immortality. He'd be forgotten, most likely, without Randolph's venom.

Ervin: That's probably true. But I think it was Samuel Butler who said, "To himself everyone is an immortal. He may know that he is going to die, but he can never know that he is dead."

95

Interviewer: Irascible old Henry L. Mencken defined immortality this way: "The condition of a dead man who doesn't believe he is dead."

Ervin: Well, Mencken may know by now, since he's been dead some years, but I lean more to John Milton than to Mencken:

"Weep no more, woeful Shepherds, weep no more,
For Lycidas, your sorrow, is not dead,
Sunk though he be beneath the watery floor.
So sinks the day-star in the Ocean bed,
And yet Anon repairs his drooping head,
And tricks his beams, with new-spangled Ore,
Flames in the forehead of the morning sky."

Interviewer: Two or three years after the Civil War, General Lee was in Richmond, at the Spotswood Hotel. John S. Mosby, the famous ranger, had been over to pay his respects, and on the over-head passage-way, the bridge across the street between the Spotswood Hotel and the Exchange Hotel, Mosby ran into General George Pickett.

Mosby told Pickett that Lee was in his room, at the Spotswood, if Pickett wanted to pay his respects to his former commander. Apparently, Pickett resented Lee, and he railed out at "that old man who massacred my fine division at Gettysburg."

Mosby smiled: "Even if that were true, he still made you immortal, Pickett."

Ervin: Back to put-downs again for a moment. Captain Buck Kitchin, the father of Congressman Claude Kitchin, of Will Kitchin, Congressman and Governor, and father of Dr. Thurmond Kitchin, president of Wake

Forest College, was about as tempestuous as any campaigner the Democrats ever had. In eighteen eighty-two he made a speech in Minor's Warehouse in Oxford. Someone asked him what he thought of Grover Cleveland, then Governor of New York. "I think," the Captain sizzled, "that Grover Cleveland is a damn son-of-a-bitch."

Two years later, in eighteen eighty-four, when the Democrats nominated Cleveland for President, Captain Kitchin returned to Minor's warehouse where he made a rousing speech asking the people to vote for Cleveland. A man in the audience interrupted to ask: "Hold on, Captain Kitchin. Two years ago you stood on that same platform and told us Grover Cleveland is a damn son-of-a-bitch. Now, sir, you ask us to vote for him?"

The Captain stuck out his chest, nodded his head, and practically bellowed: "Yes, two years ago I said Grover Cleveland was a son-of-a-bitch, and I still say he is a son-of-a-bitch, but now, sir, he is OUR son-of-a-bitch and we have to stick to him."

A while back I told about Billy Hallyburton's succumbing to the Populists. Apparently Captain Kitchin suffered this same aberration, but only temporarily. He is supposed to have said if the Populists nominated a "yaller dog" for a certain office, he'd vote for him. Later on, when Captain Kitchin repudiated the candidate, some heckler asked if he hadn't said he'd support a "yaller dog" if the Populists nominated one.

The Captain cogitated and came back: "I did say that, and I still stick to it, but lower than a yaller dog I shall not be dragged."

Interviewer: Isn't Kitchin the man who attended the funeral services of a politician, one really raw day, was asked, "How was the funeral?" and came back, "The most lovely sight you ever saw. One infamous son-of-a-bitch was buried and about three hundred equally infamous sons-of-bitches stood with their hats off to catch pneumonia?"

Ervin: I think "Red Buck" Bryant, long-time newspaperman and Washington correspondent, told that story, about someone. It was "Red Buck," among others, who told the story about Zeb Vance's being on a boat down at Morehead City. Vance started up a ladder, from one deck to a deck above. A lady was standing on the deck up, straight above Vance, and she saw him looking up. "Huh," she grimaced, "I can tell you are no gentleman." Vance smiled, "Yes, I can tell you aren't either."

Interviewer: I knew a fellow who was so solemn-looking, so incredibly reticent, I think nature intended him to be a professional pall-bearer. He clerked in a dry goods store, and this woman, a regular customer, gave him hell for years. He never did anything to suit her, but she never went to another clerk. One day she accused him of cheating her a penny on some purchase. Very quietly he said, "Madam, when you go home, don't forget to unleash your mother in time for supper."

Ervin: "Sugar Jim" Smith, who had been a United States Senator from New Jersey, was sure Woodrow Wilson would reappoint him to the Senate when Wilson became governor, when the Democrats came back to power in New Jersey. Of course, Wilson had no idea of recommending "Sugar Jim" Smith, but Smith got an appointment with Wilson to argue the matter. When Smith was convinced Wilson wasn't going to help him, he stuck out his tongue and said, "You're no gentleman."

"And you, sir, are no judge," Wilson replied.

Interviewer: Do you know what Walter Savage Landor, the British poet, said about the Georges?

Ervin: No. Say it, please.

Interviewer:

"George the First was always reckoned
Vile, but viler George the Second.
And what mortal ever heard
Any good of George the Third?
When from earth the Fourth descended
God be praised, the Georges ended."

Ervin: Your story about the clerk in the dry-goods store is like the obstreperous drunk who kept calling the bartender a "mick." The bartender ignored the drunk for a while but finally said to him, softly, "Your younger sister is an only child." And on a higher plane there is the true story about Lady Nancy Astor and Winston Churchill. Lady Astor said to Churchill, "If I were your wife, I'd put poison in your high-ball." Without hesitating Churchill flashed back, "And if I were your husband, I'd drink it."

Interviewer: Yes, sir. Lady Astor's father, Chiswell Dabney Langhorne, a relative of Mark Twain, was our first singing tobacco auctioneer. When Langhorne started selling tobacco, the crop was relatively small and tobacco was sold a hogshead at a time. That would be around one thousand pounds in a hogshead. But the expansions of the tobacco industry necessitated the warehouse sale, with tobacco graded, as to type, and placed in individual baskets, such as is still done.

99

But no one had evolved a sing-song, the five-gaited patter that enables a tobacco auctioneer to sell about as fast as he walks. Auctioneers were still using the slow, cumbersome style of the land-auctioneer, the livestock auctioneer. Then one day when Langhorne was visiting in Richmond, a friend took him to a Roman church service, and Langhorne got the idea for the modern auctioneer's sing-song from hearing the Gregorian chant. And this format has been used by tobacco auctioneers ever since.

Ervin: That's right. Lady Astor came from Danville, Virginia.

Interviewer: Winston Churchill's telling Lady Astor, "If I were your husband, I'd drink it," reminds me of the time a woman sent Walter Hines Page a voluminous manuscript. She glued a few of the pages together, near the middle of her manuscript. When Page rejected her book, her manuscript, she wrote him a hot letter. She said Page hadn't read her opus because the pages she had glued were still stuck together. His letter of reply contained one sentence: "Madam, one does not have to eat the whole of an egg to know it is rotten."

Ervin: Page was one of our most able men, a brilliant writer and editor, and he was Woodrow Wilson's ambassador to England.

Interviewer: I believe he is the only man ever to serve as editor of the *Atlantic Monthly* who wasn't a Harvard alumnus.

Ervin: Page went to Trinity College, when it was still in Randolph County, years before it became Duke University.

Interviewer: Yes sir, there and to Randolph-Macon. Page Auditorium, at Duke, is named for him. Insofar as I know, he was the first Tar Heel to write that one of our chief economic and social handicaps was fear of domination by the Negro. Our local climate wasn't receptive to Page's advanced ideas and he went to New York, in the eighteen nineties, I think.

Ervin: That's correct. He preached that the fear of domination by blacks was developed as a political gimmick, and it did become a powerful emotional force in many old campaigns. And Page may have been the first Tar Heel to apply the phrase "priest-ridden" to Protestant mores. He wrote and spoke a lot about what he thought was the danger of ultra religious orthodoxy, but I suppose Page's ultimate "apostasy" was his repeated assertions that undue political deference was given to those who had held high rank in the Confederate army.

Interviewer: There was the campaign for clerk-of-the-court in Union County. Three candidates spoke from the same platform. The incumbent, a one-armed Confederate veteran, devoid of any legal training, told the voters that losing his arm at Gettysburg entitled him to keep the job forever.

The second candidate, equally as bereft of legal education, was a one-legged Confederate veteran, and he said he had never had an office, but that losing his leg at Cold Harbor gave him every right to have a good-paying sinecure.

The third candidate, a young lawyer, a graduate of the University, apologized because he hadn't been born at the time of the Civil War. He never mentioned his legal education, but he pointed to his shabby suit and genteel poverty. He ended with this burst of sincerity: "I'm humiliated that I didn't lose an arm, like Captain Brown lost, and I am mortified that I couldn't lose a leg, like Captain Smith lost, but for whatever it is worth, my

101

dear friends, I have the biggest damned hernia in Union County."

Ervin: There's no doubt about the fact that many various war veterans, here and elsewhere, have tried to trade in on their military contributions. I think the classic rejoinder was made by John Allen, of Mississippi, in a race for Congress against General Quitman. These two men had a joint-debate, and General Quitman spoke for two hours solely about his activities as a Confederate general. He is supposed to have mentioned the word "general" as many as a hundred times.

Then John Allen got up and here's all he said: "General Quitman was, as he said so many times, a great general. I was a lowly private in the Confederate army. Now, everyone who was a general will please vote for General Quitman and everyone who was a private can feel at home by voting for me."

Allen became known as "Private John Allen" across the whole country. Of course, he beat General Quitman, and he stayed in Congress a long time. Until the end of his days he was known as "Private John Allen" by citizens and he was always tagged "Private John Allen" in the press.

Interviewer: Wasn't a lot of campaigning done in and around saloons?

Ervin: Yes, and in the days before women got the vote, bartenders frequently had tremendous political influence.

Interviewer: You mean they gave free whiskey and free lunches to men who were pledged to their candidate?

Ervin: Yes, and in virtually every town some saloons were known, explicitly, as "Democratic" or

102

"Republican" saloons. Such places had definite political clienteles.

Interviewer: And candidates frequented these places, too?

Ervin: Oh, my, yes, they certainly did. Mr. Frank Watson, a dry and a most eloquent old-time lawyer of Burnsville, told me he heard a candidate quote Oliver Goldsmith in a saloon in Marion, North Carolina.

Interviewer: You mean the same Oliver Goldsmith who wrote *The Deserted Village, The Vicar of Wakefield,* and *She Stoops To Conquer?*

Ervin: The very same.

Interviewer: How does it go?

Ervin:

"Let schoolmasters puzzle their brain,
With grammar and nonsense and learning'
Good liquor, I soutly maintain,
Gives genius a better discerning."

Interviewer: I imagine the man made a hit.

Ervin: He did, and then some.

Interviewer: Do you remember the famous "White Ribbon" campaign, when North Carolina voted whiskey out?

Ervin: Yes, I was a small boy at the time, but the emotional tremors enveloped the whole state.

Interviewer: Those who were opposed to the "demon rum" wore white ribbons to show their purity?

Ervin: Well, the women, many of them, wore white ribbons and so did many of their children. For the first time in history women and children stood in front of saloons to campaign against whiskey.

103

Interviewer: I guess there was heavy traffic through the back doors of saloons. By the way, was this in nineteen eight?

Ervin: Yes, and, as you surmised, much thirsty trade entered through the back. It was not uncommon to see some thirsty pilgrim round the corner to his favorite saloon and then, abruptly, encounter a gang of women and children, all handing out temperance tracks and all wearing white ribbons. The fellow would keep right on walking as if he didn't know the saloon existed, right on around the other corner, down the alley, and into the back door.

Interviewer: Wasn't there some kind of "White Ribbon" chant or campaign song? I mean something almost as indigenous as "Happy Days Are Here Again," with F.D.R., or "East Side, West Side," with Al Smith?

Ervin: Yes, siree, you can bet there was. But let me interrupt to say that one of the finest, most contagious campaign songs, tunes ever associated with a man, was Champ Clark's "Houn' Dog Song," which all his followers sang in nineteen twelve when he came so close to being nominated for President.

Interviewer: That would be John Beauchamp Clark, the Speaker of the House, the man from Missouri? How does it go?

Ervin:

"Now everytime I come to town
The boys all kick my dawg aroun';
Now I don't care if he is a houn',
You better stop kicking my dawg aroun'."

Interviewer: More than a good five cent nickel the country needs a paragraph free of cliches. But, anyway, I saw a woman, really "dripping in diamonds," get out of a limousine driven by a chauffeur in uniform. In her arms she carried the smallest dog I ever saw. This fellow who was coming along the street paused, abruptly, and acted as if he were seeing an optical illusion. He regained his equipoise sufficiently to tip his hat, and he said: "Lady, I'll be damned if you ain't almost out of dog."

Ervin: Yes. Boswell in his famous *Life of Samuel Johnson*, says he told Johnson how one morning he dropped in on a meeting of Quakers where he heard a woman preach, a real rarity in the eighteenth century. Johnson answered, "Sir, a woman's preaching is like a dog's walking on his hinder legs. It is not done well; but you are surprised to find it done at all." But let me hasten to say that what Johnson said about lady preachers wouldn't be applicable today.

Interviewer: Johnson's saying he is "surprised" to find it done at all reminds me of the apocryphal story of his wife's coming home unexpectedly and catching Johnson's kissing the maid. She said, "I am surprised," and Johnson answered, "No, madam, I am surprised and you are astounded."

This may be a cliche, from over-use; but on the subject of dogs, I still revere Mark Twain's, "If you pick up a starving dog and make him prosperous, he will not bite you. This is the principal difference between a dog and a man."

Ervin: E.N. Wescotte, probably forgotten today, wrote a famous novel, *David Harum*, and David Harum, once one of our most famous fictional characters, said, "A certain number of fleas is good fer a dog – keeps him from broodin' over bein' a dog."

Interviewer: Alexander Pope used a dog for a classic denigration, or libel when, in fancy, he fashioned this couplet for the collar of the Prince of Wales' dog. The prince had his residence at Kew, and Pope wrote:

"I am his Highness' dog at Kew;
Pray tell me, Sir, whose dog are you."

But, I think we've taught old dogs enough tricks for the present. So now sing us the "White Ribbon" song.

Ervin: Sing?

Interviewer: Sing on. As the bard put it, "Warble, child; make passionate my sense of hearing."

Ervin: I think it was George Bernard Shaw, some British writer, who said, "What's too silly to be said can be sung." I'll sing or say some. But remember in this famous song a girl is telling her former sweetheart why she kicked him:

"You are coming to woo me, but not as of yore,
When I hastened to welcome your ring at the door;
For I trusted that he who stood waiting me then,
Was the brightest, the truest, the noblest of men;
Your lips, on my own, when they printed 'Farewell,'
Had never been soiled by the beverage of hell;
But they come to me with the bacchanal sign;
And the lips that touch liquor shall never touch
    mine."

Interviewer: I imagine the ambiguity of that last line was derided by some wet scofflaws and dastards. But that's how "Lips that touch liquor shall never touch mine" got started?

106

Ervin: You are right on both counts. There was some "lewd sneering," among fellows of the "baser sort." Yes, many girls extracted solemn promises from their beaux, relative to the boys' lips touching liquor. I don't know how many adhered to the pledge, but I think the result showed up in the ballot-box, even if it was violated at what came to be called the "blind-tiger."

Interviewer: "Blind tiger" was a euphemism for illicit whiskey?

Ervin: Yes.

Interviewer: I suppose this tale, told to me by the late Sam Wheeler, Sheriff of Granville County, involves a "blind tiger," of sorts. The Sheriff said that after North Carolina voted out whiskey in nineteen eight, there was a ruling, or, perhaps, an understanding, that farmers could use their surplus corn, apples, and grapes for whiskey, brandy, and wine; but this had to be used for home-consumption, exclusively, for neighborhood illnesses and that sort of thing.

Sometime after nineteen eight Sheriff Wheeler heard that two boys, brothers, in the Knap-of-Reeds section of Granville County, were using most of their "surplus" corn and apples to ship whiskey and brandy in barrels on the railroad to such far, exotic places as Henderson and Durham, North Carolina.

Ervin: The barrels contained some misleading label?

Interviewer: Yes sir, I believe most of them were marked "Molasses." Anyway, the good Sheriff felt compelled to make an investigation. So he rode in his buggy out to Knap-of-Reeds; and just as he approached the small train depot in the village, he saw these two boys, the brothers, with a two-horse wagon load of barrels. The Sheriff and the brothers reached the little

107

depot at the same time, the Sheriff from the front and the brothers from the back.

The Sheriff said to one of the brothers, pleasantly enough, "Tom, what you got in all those barrels?"

"Hits water, Sheriff."

"Whatchu you gon to do with all that water, Tom?"

"Water baccer plants, Sheriff."

"Well, I'm a mite thirsty. So I'll just have me a sup of your water." So saying, the Sheriff got the "depot dipper." He opened the taps to several of the barrels until he had filled his dipper. He took a huge swallow, and it was about one hundred fifty proof corn whiskey. The Sheriff smacked his lips and handed the dipper to the brother: "Here Tom, you have a sup, too."

The boy drank, slurped, sipped, sort of gargled, and said in a tone of abject incredulity, "Dog-gone if Jesus ain't gone and done hit again, Sheriff."

Ervin: There used to be this proverb: "If you add water to wine, it ruins it; if you don't, it ruins you."

Interviewer: That's so, but it was the late G.K. Chesterton, one of the most militant Catholic laymen of his time, who wrote:

"And Noah he often said to his wife,
when he sat down to dine,
'I don't care where the water goes,
if it doesn't get into the wine."

Ervin: You are quoting the Englishman who wrote those fine stories about the brilliant amateur detective, Father Brown?

Interviewer: Yes, sir. The first time Chesterton visited New York his host made a tremendous production of showing him Times Square at night. The host pointed to all the flashing neons and said, "Isn't this fantastic."

"It would be," Chesterton replied, "if one couldn't read."

Ervin: "Wine and women" were linked in literature and aphorisms for centuries, but Lord Byron may have been one of the first to add "mirth and laughter," in *Don Juan*:

"Let us have wine and women, mirth and laughter,
Sermons and soda-water the day after."

Interviewer: And John O'Hara used *Sermons and Soda-Water* as the title for a book of his short stories published a few years ago. Although I don't know a great deal about Martin Luther's personal habits, Thackeray may have been one of the first to bring in "song," in the ditty Thackeray wrote about Luther:

"Then sing as Martin Luther sang,
As Doctor Martin Luther sang:
'Who loves not wine, woman, and song
He is a fool his whole life long.' "

Ervin: I note that Thackeray has Luther say "woman," not "women." Someone, perhaps, "F.P.A.," the late Franklin P. Adams, said that in the order named, these are the hardest to control: Wine, women, and song.

The difference between Byron and Luther may lie in one's using "women" and one's using "woman." Hence, Thackeray sort of stole Byron's thunder.

Interviewer: Do you know how "stealing his thunder" originated?

Ervin: If so, I don't recall the origin.

Interviewer: About seventeen hundred nine, John Dennis, a somewhat inept British playwright, produced at Drury Lane his play, *Appius and Virginia*, and Dennis came up with a new way to make thunder on the stage. Previously theatrical thunder had been produced by large bowls, but Dennis made thunder by putting stops into wooden troughs. His play was a failure, and it closed after a short run.

Shortly after his play closed, Dennis went to Drury Lane to see a performance of *MacBeth*, and he was horrified to hear his new method of making thunder being appropriated for Shakespeare's play. He went charging down the aisle, leaped onto the stage and exclaimed, "That's my thunder you people hear, by God. These villians will not play my play, but, by God, they steal and rattle my thunder."

Ervin: It was Shakespeare, whom you just mentioned, who wrote, in *As You Like It*, "Good wine needs no bush."

Interviewer: Bush?

Ervin: Yes, ancient wine shops were marked by a wreath, or a bush, or wisp of hay hanging on the door. What Shakespeare is saying is that the merit of the wine, itself, attracts customers.

Interviewer: Then Shakespeare must be one of the first to refute Madison Avenue. Today, we think just the opposite, that the bush takes precedence over the wine, the product.

Ervin: I really suppose that "Good wine needs no bush" is an ancient variant of Ralph Waldo Emerson's "better mousetrap" idea, that if a man makes anything that is better, the world will beat a path to his door, no matter how inaccessible his shop may be.

110

Interviewer: That wouldn't happen today without copious advertising; and if the man didn't have some influence with his highway commissioner, he probably would play hell even getting a pig-path to his door.

Ervin: I'm afraid your points have validity. The story you told about "Jesus done it again" reminds me of a true story that happened in Salisbury many years ago. A man was accused of stealing an expensive pocket watch from a jewelry store. He said he didn't know anything about how the watch came to be in his possession, that on the night in question he had been drinking at the Mount Vernon Inn in Salisbury, and he remembered nothing after he went to the bar there.

This judge, whom I better not identify, came to Salisbury to hold court, to try the man accused of stealing the watch, among others. The night before the watch trial came up, the accused man's lawyer invited the judge to have drinks and supper with him at the old Mount Vernon Inn's bar and dining room, which adjoined each other.

The lawyer slipped the bartender a tip and the lawyer's drinks were watered down while the judge's got stronger and stronger. But the judge, who prided himself on holding his whiskey, of taking drink-to-drink with any man, emptied his glass each time it was filled. Finally, the judge went to sleep at the eating table.

While the judge snoozed, the lawyer quietly and quickly gathered up a double handful of knives, forks, spoons, and salt shakers, each of which contained the Mount Vernon Inn's crest, initials, or some identifying mark. Then the lawyer stuffed all of this silverware into the judge's overcoat pockets. When the judge aroused, the lawyer held his overcoat, and he helped 'the judge back to his own hotel.

The next morning when the judge got ready to go to the courthouse, he found all the stuff from the Mount Vernon Inn in his overcoat pockets. He couldn't imagine what had happened, and, in a cold sweat, he had wild thoughts of having been a sleep-walking kleptomaniac the dreadful night before.

Smitten with a hangover, a terrible sense of guilt, and enveloped in grimmest consternation, the poor judge plodded on to court, to hear the case of the man accused of stealing the watch. When the defendant testified that he remembered nothing that happened after he went to the bar of the Mount Vernon Inn, the judge shouted down to the solicitor: "Mr. Solicitor, I want prayer for judgment continued in this case. All the circumstances are extenuating. Any man who drinks that damned liquor at the Mount Vernon Inn isn't responsible for anything he does afterward.

Interviewer: George Ade, the humorist and short story writer, wasn't a poet but he got off some good lines about a hangover. It's called "Remorse":

"A dark brown taste, a burning thirst,
A head that's ready to split and burst.
No time for mirth, no time for laughter,
The cold gray dawn of the morning after."

Ervin: I guess Brother George was doing what is called "writing from experience" today. The late Gregg Cherry, Governor of North Carolina from nineteen forty-five to forty-nine, used to tell this story on himself. Before he was governor, Cherry was met on the streets of Gastonia by a stranger who needed a lawyer. "Who's the best lawyer in town?" the man asked him.

112

Cherry replied, "Gregg Cherry, when he isn't drunk."

The stranger came back: "Then, who's the second-best lawyer in town?"

"Greg Cherry, when he's drunk."

Interviewer: At a Southern Governors' Conference Cherry was seated beside Strom Thurmond, then Governor of South Carolina. Thurmond kept chatting, talking to Cherry, but Cherry ate on and confined his responses to a few grunts and nods. Finally, Thurmond said: "Governor Cherry, I don't believe you like me?"

Cherry turned his head: "I haven't thought about it much, one way or the other. But if you have to have an answer you can wire your folks and tell 'em I'm no damned fool about you, Strom."

Ervin: Was it Eugene Field, the poet, who said there are two reasons for drinking: One is, when you are thirsty, to cure it; the other, when you are not thirsty, to prevent it?

Interviewer: I don't know, Senator, but Field was a brilliant wit and a clever dramatic and musical critic; although most people knew him, and remember him, if they remember him at all, as the man who wrote such ultra sentimental verses as "Little Boy Blue." He was a crack newspaper, one of the early columnists, in St. Louis, Denver, and Chicago.

Ervin: He didn't live long, did he?

Interviewer: No, sir. He was forty-five, when he died in eighteen ninety-five. Here's a review he wrote in Chicago of a performance by the Budapest Stringed Quartet: "Last night the Budapest Stringed Quartet played Brahms. Brahms lost."

Ervin: That was his whole review?

Interviewer: Yes, sir, and this is how he reviewed a

play called *Dreadful Night*: *"Dreadful Night*: Precisely."

Ervin: I heard a story about how Field, who had a persistent fondness for the grape, ran up a large tab at his favorite saloon in St. Louis. The proprietor knew Field made a modest salary, had a large family, and the proprietor was abundantly protective about Field's poetic sensibilities. He wanted to erase Field's considerable debt, but he wanted the matter handled with consummate delicacy. Now, Christmas was at hand, and he thought of this innocuous device:

He gathered Field's mountain of bar-chits into a neat pile, wrapped them in white paper marked "Paid In Full," and gave the bundle to Field for a Christmas present.

Field accepted the bundle, rapped the polished bar with his knuckles and said to the proprietor: "And, now, Pat, let me have my mandatory double-bourbon."

"Your what, Mr. Field?"

"Pat, is it not a rule in every saloon that when a man pays his account in full he gets a double drink on the house?"

Interviewer: Field was no Poe or Whitman, but every Christmastime when rapt expectancy is a marvelous fever in my bones, I start to chanting:

"Mother calls me William, Father calls me Will,
Sister calls me Willie, but the fellers call me Bill:
Now all the whole year round there ain't no flies
    on me,
But jess afore Christmas I'm ez good ez I kin be."

Ervin: I knew you were going to say that before you said it. There's really no close connection, but it reminds me of James Whitcomb Riley's poem about the "gobble-uns." Can you say it?

114

Interviewer: Riley called it "Little Orphant Annie," and inadvertently, he supplied the name for an interminable comic strip. I can say part of it, in broken doses, if that's o.k.

Ervin: Any way will be fine. I haven't heard it for years.

Interviewer:

"An' all us other children, when the supper things
    is done,
We set around the kitchen fire an' has the mostest
    fun,
A-list'nin' to the witch tales 'at Annie tells about
An' the gobble-uns 'at gits you
    Ef you
    Don't
    Watch
    Out.

"Onc't there was a little boy wouldn't say his pray'rs —
An' when he went to bed at night, away up the stairs,
His mammy heerd him holler, an' his daddy heerd
    him bawl,
An' when they turn't the kivvers down, he wasn't
    there at all!
An' they seeked him in the rafter-room, an' cubby-
    hole, an' press,
An' seeked him up the chimbly-flue, an' ever' wheres,
    I guess.
But all they ever found was thist his pants an'
    roundabout!
An' the Gobble-uns'll git you
    Ef you
    Don't
    Watch
    Out."

Ervin: But Riley was a man of some education, some learning, wasn't he? He used dialect and grammatical irregularities to come across with wide bodies of readers?

Interviewer: Exactly. He used the same essential format in rhyme that Petroleum V. Nasby, Josh Billings and others whom we've mentioned, had used in prose. As a matter of fact, Riley went to college and he studied law. He discarded Blackstone for a traveling medicine-show, and then he went around the countryside painting barns.

And he pulled one of the great literary frauds, albeit a harmless one. In eighteen eighty-two he published a poem called "Leonainie," which he wrote, in a newspaper at Kokomo, Indiana. Now, Riley wrote this poem in the style of Edgar Allan Poe, and he appended the initials "E.A.P." as author, to the poem.

Apparently, about half of the national academic community was duped by Riley's ruse. Many professors thought that the editor at Kokomo had come up with a truly sensational literary find, that he had discovered one of Poe's unpublished masterpieces. Several learned papers, pro and con, were written before Riley and the editor admitted the whole thing was a fake.

Ervin: This was a publicity stunt? Riley palmed off "Leonainie," I believe you said it was, to call attention to his own poems? You know, I still like the one you quoted, "The Old Swimming Hole," and "When the Frost Is on the Punkin," most especially.

Do you know anything about Riley, what kind of man he was?

Interviewer: Well, his poetic rustic simplicity wasn't so naive as it seems at times. I suppose he assumed most of his readers were unsophisticated, and he traded in on their emotions. As Riley wrote, he could see the reader about to smile. So, Riley broadens his joke. Then when he sees tears about to appear in the reader's eye, he turns up the pathos. But aside from the insight I get from his writing methods, I depend upon a story George Ade told. Ade and Riley were living in Indianapolis. Although Riley was much older, the two were good friends.

One delicious fall morning, Ade went by Riley's home and asked Riley to take a walk with him, to enjoy the autumn weather, to have a drink. Riley got his hat, hesitated a minute, and declined George Ade's invitation. Ade asked why?

"Well, George, before we have gone two blocks some idiot will stop me, chunk me in the ribs with his elbow, cackle like a guinea hen, and say, 'The frost is on the punkin vine, ain't it, Mr. Riley?' My damn ribs are sore already, but more to the point, I left off with 'punkin.' I never said anything about any damned vine.' "

So, Senator, from that sample I'd judge that Riley was delightfully irascible, sardonic, anyway.

Ervin: I guess Riley was almost as much a card as Eugene Field, and, as you say, Riley wasn't a great poet but there's always the smell of fall and the opulence of the harvest in "When the Frost Is on the Punkin," the red and yellow apples in the cellar, the barrels of cider, the mince pies, the apple-butter, the souse-meat and the sausages.

Interviewer: You are exactly right. Riley ends the poem, at the apogee of the harvest, by saying, having a little boy say, that if the angels wanted boarding, he'd be in splendid shape to take care of them: "I'd want to 'commodate 'em — all the whole endurin' flock —/When

117

the frost is on the punkin and the fodder's in the shock."

You know, Senator, the boy who never greeted fall in terms of burning out the chimney, in the ringing symphonies of the ax on the chopping block, in scents of apples and pears mellowing on a shelf, and in fields aflame in the moonlight with golden shocks of fodder has really danced into November with one boot off.

Ervin: Yes, our yards used to be redolent with the aroma of homemade molasses, great pots of homemade catsup, and those tremendous earthen jars that held shredded cabbage until it became sauerkraut.

Interviewer: And hardly anyone makes locust-and-persimmon beer anymore. That was delectable stuff, Senator.

Ervin: Didn't some people call it "small beer?"

Interviewer: "Small beer" was beer with low alcoholic content. "Small" didn't relate to serving glasses, as it does today. Some folks let their locust-and-persimmon beer get as hard as the cruel heart of a note-shaver, but most people used it for a family drink. It was simple to make. You put alternate rows of locusts and persimmons and broom-straw in a barrel, and then you filled the barrel with water. Many families ran off two batches, a barrel for children and temperance folks and a barrel for resolute adults. However, the relatively low alcoholic content of the "grown folks' barrel" made it "small beer."

118

IX

Ervin: I think we are doubly blessed in North Carolina in having four distinctive seasons — fall, winter, spring, and summer; and, as you say, each used to have its very own rituals and pageants, from the corn-shucking dinner in fall, to the "possum-and-taters" feasts in winter, to the shad-bake in spring, to the barbecue in summer.

The word "fodder," from the Anglo-Saxon "fodor," food-stuff for animals, which Riley mentions several times in that poem, used to be known as well in town as on the farm, but its general use has declined today.

Interviewer: Sam Jones, the famous Methodist preacher and revivalist, used "fodder" in his famous admonition to young preachers: "Gentlemen, always throw the fodder on the ground so the animals can get to it."

Ervin: Yes. Sam Jones, who died around nineteen hundred and nine, was about as effective as anyone who ever stood in a pulpit or preached from the tail-gate of a wagon. Because he had been a lawyer and a drunkard, before he got the call to preach, people said "Sam Jones is a double-devil reformed." Once, at this camp-meeting, Sam Jones was standing in front of a table loaded with pies. He whispered to a small boy standing beside him: "Son, don't take your eyes off those chess pies while I am saying grace."

Interviewer: Tell me, Senator, just what was a camp-meeting?

Ervin: It was a tremendous religious revival, held outdoors, and it seems to have started in Kentucky around eighteen hundred, with the preaching of James McCready, known as a Cumberland Presbyterian. The camp-meeting was held where church buildings didn't exist or where they were too small and too few to accommodate the crowds.

Men, women, and children came from miles around, and they camped out, for about a week, while the revival was going on. They slept in their wagons, and they had to bring sufficient provisions for the family and the horses or mules to eat. As a matter of fact, some folks brought milk cows and live chickens to the camp-meeting.

Frequently, the crowd was so large that several men preached simultaneously at various points on the camp-ground, and at other times, revivalists took turns preaching. Of course, couples were married while the camp-meeting was in session, and children were baptized and christened. I believe that most of the camp-meetings came under the direction of the Baptists, Methodists, Christians, and Cumberland Presbyterians.

Interviewer: And because of the paucity of church buildings, the immigrants took the camp-meeting to the west?

Ervin: Yes, they certainly did, but the camp-meeting

doubled-back from Kentucky to portions of North Carolina and some of the other more established states. Many camp-meetings in the last century were held in the more sparsely populated portions of North Carolina. As a matter of the fact, the camp-meeting, certainly in a modified form, lasted until the end of the last century, especially in the region between the Alleghenies and the Mississippi. But, as you suggested, the camp-meeting went west with immigrants, all the way from Kentucky to California.

Interviewer: I wonder if some immigrant at a California camp-meeting met the Californian Robert Frost described?

Ervin: I think you have me there. Who was he?

Interviewer:

"I met a Californian who would
Talk California — a state so blessed,
He said, in climate, none had ever died there
A natural death, and Vigilance Committees
Had to organize to stock the graveyards
And vindicate the state's humanity."

Ervin: But Mark Twain, who prospected for gold in California for a while, wasn't enamored with interminable life. He said: "Whoever has lived long enough to find out what life is, knows how deep a debt of gratitude we owe to Adam, the first great benefactor of our race. He brought death into the world."

Interviewer: That's one of Pudd'nhead Wilson's maxims?

Ervin: Yes, it is.

Interviewer: Despite the fact that Mark Twain

121

expressed many longings for death, he contradicted himself a little in another of Pudd'nhead's sayings: "Each person was born to one possession which outvalues all the others — his last breath."

Ervin: And he also said, "I believe that our Heavenly Father invented man because He was disappointed in the monkey."

Interviewer: And, "Wagner's music is better than it sounds." But this missionary journey we were just on, the camp-meeting days, reminds me of a story you told about a lawyer in Cherokee County.

Ervin: Yes, his name was Marshall Bell, and he thought he had an insoluble legal problem. A man in Cherokee County left some property to a Baptist Church. His will stipulated that if this Baptist Church ceased to use the property, then the land was to go "To God Almighty, or His heirs and assigns."

A larger church was built in a more central location, on a better road, and, of course, the trustees of the old property wanted to sell it, but Marshall Bell, their attorney, just couldn't find any legal way to circumvent the will, giving the land "To God Almighty, or His Heirs or assigns." Then one day Marshall Bell was in Raleigh and on Fayetteville Street he met up with Chief Justice Walter Stacy, of the North Carolina Supreme Court. As the two walked, Bell proceeded to tell about his inextricable problem. Judge Stacy smiled: "Bell, your solution is simple. When you return to Cherokee, just run a notice in your newspaper in which you state, officially, that neither 'God Almighty or His heirs or assigns can be found in Cherokee County.' After you do that, draw your deed and convey the property."

Interviewer: The lawyer, Bell, did that?

Ervin: Yes, of course, Marshall Bell and many of the other folks in Cherokee County took a ribbing about living in a place beyond the pale.

Interviewer: "Pale," originally, is from the Latin "palus," and meant a stake, didn't it, Senator?

Ervin: Yes, that's right. Then from about the twelfth to the seventeenth centuries, a pale was a territory in Ireland controlled by the English.

Interviewer: Your Cherokee story about God Almighty reminds me of one I heard the late Chief Justice William A. Devin tell. A man in Tennessee named George W. Hell claimed title to property on which a Baptist church had been built. Hell won in the lower court, but the trustees appealed the case to the Tennessee Supreme Court. The higher court over-ruled the lower court, and the justice who wrote the majority opinion concluded his brief with this statement: "The court holds, therefore, that this Baptist church may not go to Hell."

I believe Hatcher Hughes wrote a play called *Hell-Bent For Glory*, or something like that. Do you know how "hell-bent," in modern context, originated?

Ervin: I recall that as the play's title, and "Hell-bent" emerged from the campaign of eighteen forty, in Maine. A man named Edward Kent said he was "Hell-bent for election," as governor of Maine. Kent won, and his party, the Whigs, celebrated their victory with this song:

"Oh, have you heard how old Maine went?
She went hell-bent for Governor Kent
And Tippacanoe and Tyler, too."

123

Interviewer: "Hell-bent-for-election" endures in several areas, but one rarely ever hears "From Hull, Hell and Halifax, Good God, deliver us."

Ervin: How did that start?

Interviewer: My understanding, Senator, it was a beggar's chant, in England. All three places had bad reputations, certainly from the vagrant's standpoint. Apparently, the town of Hull had stringent ordinances against all forms of vagrancy, and Halifax was credited with two terrible expedients. "Halifax law" was said to mean that a man was executed and then tried. And those who were executed were decapitated. According to the story, Halifax had an insturment much like the infamous guillotine, but long before the guillotine was known by that name.

I believe that "From Hull, Hell, and Halifax, Good Lord, deliver us," is in Thomas Fuller's writings, of the seventeenth century. Apparently, the beggars developed their own litany, and they wanted no more of Hull, Hell, and Halifax than bums of a future generation wanted railroad dicks who carried big sticks.

Ervin: That explains why many people used to use "Go to Halifax" as a mild euphemism. But it's interesting that the British beggars put "Hull ahead of "hell."

Interviewer: Well, I suppose some of them had had the misfortune to go to Hull but could merely speculate about hell.

Ervin: I suppose so. Incidentally, it was Philip Sheridan, not General Sherman, as many contend, who said, "If I owned Texas and Hell I would rent out Texas and live in Hell." Apparently, Sheridan made the observation when he was a young lieutenant on duty in

Texas around eighteen fifty-five. Then when he became a famous Civil War general, the crack was revived. But this whole thing about Texas and hell may have started with Davy Crockett. When Crockett was defeated for Congress, in Tennessee, in eighteen thirty-four, he wrote in his autobiography: "I put the ingredients in the cup pretty strong, I tell you, and I concluded my speech by telling them that I had done with politics for the present, that the voters could go to hell, and I would go to Texas."

Interviewer: Yes, sir. I believe "Hell and Texas" was a bland term of profanity throughout much of the last century. By the way, Senator, did you know the devil was banished, officially, from Gates County, North Carolina?

Ervin: I remember something about his satanic majesty's being banished from one of our eastern counties, but I have forgotten the details. What happened?

Interviewer: In the days before the Revolutionary War the devil won a lot of money in Eastern Carolina betting on horse races. Whenever there was a race, the devil camouflaged himself with a long, jim-swinger coat, a fancy vest, and beaver hat. He could conjure the horse with his eyes, make the horse run fast this way. The devil tried this trick after the war, when Gates was created, and he was so successful in conjuring the horse that the horse ran straight towards the devil's hypnotic eyes. The horse ran over the devil, knocked off his beaver hat, ripped his jim-swinger coat. Thus, he was revealed in all his horns, cloven feet and the rest.

The devil wasn't tarred and feathered but he was ridden out of Gates County on a rail, and he was banished, by a committee of prominent citizens, under threat of serious retaliation, if he ever returned to Gates County. This was in seventeen eighty-five and the devil hasn't been back yet, to Gates County, I mean.

Ervin: That recalls the fellow who was tarred and feathered and ridden out of town on a rail. Near the corporate limit, some wiseacre along the sidewalk hollered to the man: "Hey, fellow, how you like your ride?"

"Well, I'll tell you, if it weren't for the honor of the damn thing, I'd just as soon walk."

Interviewer: People don't talk about the devil nearly so much as they did in insular days, and we hardly ever call him Mr. Scratch, Old Nick, or even Satan today.

Ervin: You are exactly right. I think "Mr. Scratch" is an Americanism, basically, and I believe it was used in the early days of the colonies, when Mr. Scratch, or satan, was likely to be endowed with many of the personal attributes of the man down the road, the meanest, most diabolically crafty man down the road. I believe "Mr. Scratch" is used in Washington Irving's famous story, "The Devil and Tom Walker," published around eighteen hundred.

Interviewer: That's true, and, of course, the late Stephen Vincent Benet used Mr. Scratch as Daniel Webster's adversary in "The Devil and Daniel Webster," published thirty-odd years and dramatized several times on television and elsewhere.

Ervin: Yes, and Daniel Webster and the folks in Gates County were unique in besting the devil.

Interviewer: One might say both beat hell out of the devil. But the devil gets the short end of the stick in one of Hilaire Belloc's delicious, but, meanly forgotten, epigrams:

126

"The Devil, having nothing else to do,
Went off to tempt My Lady Poltagrue.
My Lady, tempted by a private whim,
To his extreme annoyance, tempted him"

I think you'll agree that Old Nick was the prevalent term in North Carolina, and there used to be a theory that "Nick," in this connotation, came from Niccolo Machiavelli (1429-1527).

Ervin: Well, many high-minded statesmen, including Thomas Jefferson, thought Machiavelli was a real prince of darkness.

Interviewer: Yes sir, and his frequent movements were said to be so swift, devious, and elusive that his mail was addressed to him, "Wherever the devil he may be."

Ervin: Satan, which usually managed to evoke the image of the snake in our society, has a tricky sort of etymology. Although "satan" occurs many, many times in the Old Testament, "satan" is translated as an "adversary," an evil spirit, "the adversary of God and man," in only three references, in Zechariah, Chronicles, and Job.

Interviewer: In *King Lear*, I think it is, Shakespeare says, "The prince of darkness is a gentleman." Was he a gentleman very often, Senator?

Ervin: Oh, yes, he certainly was, but this was probably in deference to his previous status as an archangel, when he was also called Lucifer. Isaiah writes, "How art thou fallen from heaven, O Lucifer, son of the morning!" And in *Paradise Lost*, John Milton gives this vivid picture:

"High on a throne of royal state, which far
Outshone the wealth of Ormus and of Ind,
Or where the gorgeous East with richest hand
Showers on her kings barbaric pearl and gold
Satan exalted sat, by merit rais'd."

Interviewer: "Ind" and Ormus," Senator?

Ervin: "Ind" means India, and "Ormus" is a word Milton used to mean the East.

Interviewer: Someone is bound to have theorized that the devil became a gentleman in the eyes of destitute European peasants. The devil was high-born, had fallen from heaven, and it was natural for the impoverished peasant to see all high-born men as wicked. Wickedness sort of went along with power, wealth, and station. I suppose the peasant thought the high-born were as wicked, wicked on a grandiose scale, as he would be if he had the opportunity. But, whatever the reason, the devil always spoke Norman French in the old "Morality Plays," and until fairly recently he wore a high hat, white tie, and an opera cape. So he probably came across much the same as the "dissolute English gentleman turned cad" in some of the nineteenth century melodramas.

Ervin: Yes, but you can't imagine the devil in a tuxedo or in a white linen suit.

Interviewer: No, sir. Robert Burns may have been among the first in literature to give the devil his familiar trappings, although Burns calls him a "towzie tyke," a shaggy, vagrant dog, and not a goat:

"A winnock-bunker in the east,
There sat auld Nick, in shape o' beast;
A towzie tyke, black, grim, and large."

Tell me, Senator, did the once-celebrated "Neck Verse" have anything to do with the devil?

Ervin: No, not to my knowledge. The so-called "Neck verse" appears in Chronicles, 16:22, "Touch not mine annointed ones, and do my prophets no harm." Anyone who could stand and read that verse in a British Court, and later in many local courts, was "entitled to benefit of clergy." Now, here's what had happened: Originally "benefit of clergy" was a privilege extended to ministers which excluded them from trial by a secular court, if they were arraigned for a felony.

Such clergymen were tried, instead, by Ecclesiastical courts, and since Ecclesiastical courts did not give the death sentence, the accused's life was saved by this process. Ultimately, "benefit of clergy" was extended to literate laymen who could read the verse from Chronicles.

However, a man could not plead the "Neck verse" a second time. After he used it once, he was branded in the hand.

Interviewer: Like having his ticket punched on an oldtime day-coach?

Ervin: That's it. Interestingly enough, the "Neck verse," "benefit of clergy," was extended to women in England, in sixteen ninety or ninety-one, I believe. The custom was abolished in England in eighteen twenty-seven, and I believe all American courts abolished the custom about that time, too.

Interviewer: Well, the "Neck verse" did apply to the devil, in the sense that literacy allowed some people to "beat the devil around the stump." But, many thanks for your explanation. I had heard that "Rare Ben" Jonson claimed the "Neck verse" to escape hanging for killing a man in a duel. I was puzzled by the allusion, and I am grateful to the "high court" for the excellent elucidation.

Ervin: Samuel Pepys, in a diary note of sixteen hundred and sixty, has this quixical observation: "I went out to Charing Cross to see Major Harrison hanged, drawn, and quartered; which was done there, he being as cheerful as any man could do in that condition."

Interviewer: Harrison was in "great shape, for the fix he was in." Your Pepys story and your story about the hanging of Tom Dula remind me of Jonathan Swift's ballad about the hanging of Tom Clinch:

"Clever Tom Clinch, while the rabble was bawling,
Rode stately through Holborn to die at his calling.
He stopt at the George for a bottle of sack,
And promis'd to pay for it when he came back."

As I understand it, one had to pass through Holborn to reach the gallows, located at Tyburn. Public hangings were tremendous spectacles then, during the seventeenth century, and custom gave the doomed man some small favors along the way, like the "last big meal" here. Swift seems to say that the victim was greatly admired if he went to the gallows with some bravado, some swagger.

Ervin: Yes, that's true. And on a higher plane there is the story about Sir Thomas More's execution. As Sir Thomas ascended the scaffold he said to his military escort: "I pray you, Master Lieutenant, see me up safe, and for my coming down let me shift for myself."

Interviewer: A cheap hood, hopped up on something, pulled a gun on a friend of mine, and a couple of other folks. The hood told my friend if he didn't submit to certain slight indignities, he would shoot him. My friend answered, "Then you may as well start shooting. If I'm to be intimidated by a son-of-a-bitch like you, I'd be better off dead."

Ervin: Was your friend shot?

Interviewer: No, sir. He put some pipe tobacco in his mouth, chewed it, or gummed it, until he had a mouth filled with amber. He spat the amber in the hood's eyes, kicked him below the belt, took the pistol away from him, made a citizen's arrest, and delivered the hood to the police station.

Ervin: Our somewhat morbid preoccupation with hanging and dying reminds me that the eloquent death-bed statement seems to have vanished. Daniel Webster's whole family was in the room, along with the doctor and some neighbors, as he lay dying. Webster lapsed into a coma; but when he regained consciousness, he exclaimed: Wife, children, physician, neighbors, did I, in my delirium, say anything that is unbecoming to the name of Daniel Webster?"

Interviewer: Many of the oldtimers seem to have spent their last moments polishing their curtain speeches. I think Heine, the poet, got off one of the best, when he died in eighteen fifty-six. A priest had just told Heine that God would forgive his sins. "Why, of course, He will forgive me; that's His business."

Ervin: I think it was Henry Ward Beecher who said, "I can forgive, but I cannot forget is only another way saying I cannot forgive."

Interviewer: That's right, but Beecher forgot that forgetting is not an act of volition. I imagine it was such continued preaching as this that made golf so popular on Sunday morning.

Now, this has absolutely no pertinence to anything

we're talking about, but Karl Marx's mother got off one of my favorite aphorisms: "If my son, Karl, instead of writing a lot about capital, had made a lot of capital, it would have been much better."

Ervin: Excellent, capital, I might add, and that reminds me of something Thackeray has Becky Sharp say in *Vanity Fair*: "I think I could be a good woman if I had five thousand a year."

Interviewer: She's talking about pounds?

Ervin: Yes.

Interviewer: That would be around twenty-five thousand dollars a year, back in Becky's time. I may not have been good but I have been law-abiding on a whole lot less.

Scott Fitzgerald, exuding lofty disdain, bragged to Ernest Hemingway, "We are different from the rich folks."

"Yes, I know," Hemingway replied, "They have more money."

Ervin: Kin Hubbard put it this way: "When a man keeps hollering, 'It's the principle of the thing,' he's talking about the money."

Interviewer: Wasn't Kin Hubbard a contemporary of "Mr. Dooley," and didn't the two use similar formats?

Ervin: I think Kin Hubbard, Frank McKinney, died in nineteen thirty, at about seventy-two, and "Mr. Dooley," actually Finley Peter Dunne, died in nineteen thirty-six, around seventy. Hubbard spoke often through his alter-ego, or Charlie McCarthy, a character he called "Abe Martin." Finley Peter Dunne spoke through conversations "Mr. Dooley" had with his favorite bartender, Hennessey.

Kin Hubbard said, "About the only thing we have

that actually discriminates in favor of the plain people is the stork." And he had Abe Martin to say: "It's no disgrace to be poor, but it might as well be."

Interviewer: Hubbard's crack about the stork reminds me of this: The last thing Bat Masterson wrote was: "There is a general equality in nature. Take ice. In summer the rich get all the ice they want, and in winter the poor get more than they want."

Ervin: Masterson worked for the *Washington Evening Star*, didn't he?

Interviewer: I believe so, and other newspapers, perhaps. Despite the impression that the famous television series gave, when Masterson was played by Gene Barry, I believe he was a western marshall a relatively short while.

Ervin: I think he was appointed marshall by Teddy Roosevelt.

Interviewer: Yes sir, and he lived until around nineteen twenty-four, and, according, to the story, his words about ice were found in his typewriter at his death.

Now, Senator, my Irish accent is pretty bad but wasn't it "Mr. Dooley," Finley Peter Dunne, who said: "A fanatic is a man that does what he thinks th' Lord wud do if He knew th' true facts iv th' case?"

Ervin: He did, and it was Winston Churchill who said, "A fanatic is one who can't change his mind and won't change the subject."

Interviewer: And "Mr. Dooley" said, "I care not who makes th' laws iv a nation if I can get out an injunction."

Ervin: And long ago, when people were likely to think the United States Supreme Court was almost .

sacrosanct, he wrote, "No matther whether the' constitution follows th' flag or not, the supreme court follows th' iliction returns."

Interviewer: At the apogee of a so-called national crusade against alleged vice, "Dooley" put the whole damn business into proper focus: "Vice is a creature of such hejees mien that th' more ye see it th' betther you like it."

Ervin: I think Dunne got that from a portion of Alexander Pope's "Essay on Man." And it may have been Seneca who wrote, "We bear with those vices we are accustomed to; we reprove new ones."

Interviewer: And Seneca anticipated "R" and "X" rated by almost two thousand years when he observed, "What were once vices are now the manners of the day."

But, then, again, "Mr. Dooley" made a vibrant point when he said: "Th' past always looks betther thin it was. It's only pleasant because it isn't here anymore."

Ervin: There's much to that, and there's much to Dunne's observation, made at a time when age and wisdom were likely to be synonomous in many parts of this country: "Many a man that cudden't direct ye to th' drug store on th' corner whin he was thirty will get a respectful hearin' whin age has further impaired his mind." Or, perhaps, the older man can give excellent advice and precepts because he can't give bad examples.

Interviewer: Shakespeare said, "My age is as a lusty winter,/Frosty, but kindly." Now, I don't give a dried apple dam if some self-winding esthete puts down Lord Tennyson, but I was brought up on "Ulysses," and I am glad, everyday of my life, I had to learn the last part of the poem by heart.

Ervin: Good for you. Let's hear it.

134

Interviewer:

"Old age hath yet his honor and his toil.
Death closes all, but something ere the end,
Some work of noble note, may yet be done,
Not unbecoming men that strove with Gods.
The lights begin to twinkle from the rocks;
The long day wanes; the slow moon climbs; the deep
Moans round with many voices. Come, my friends,
"Tis not too late to seek a newer world.
Push off, and sitting well in order smite
The sounding furrows; for my purpose holds
To sail beyond the sunset, and the baths
Of all the western stars, until I die.
It may be that gulfs will wash us down;
It may be we shall touch the Happy Isles
And see the great Achilles, whom we knew.
Tho' much is taken, much abides; and tho'
We are not that strength which in old days
Moved earth and heaven, that which we are, we are, —
One equal temper of heroic hearts,
Made weak by time and fate, but strong in will
To strive, to seek, to find, and not to yield."

Ervin: Fine, and I'd like to say Robert Browning's
"Prospice," which means "look forward":

"Fear death — to feel the fog in my throat,
The mist in my face,
When the snows begin, and the blasts denote
I am nearing the place,
The power of the night, the press of the storm,
The post of the foe:

Where he stands, the Arch Fear in a visible form,
Yet the strong man must go;
For the journey is done and the summit attained,
And the barriers fall,
Though a battle's to fight ere the guerdon ne gained,
The reward of it all.
I was ever a fighter, so — one fight more,
The best and last!

I would hate that death bandaged my eyes, and forbore,
And bade him creep past.
No! let me taste the whole of it, fare like my peers,
The heroes of old,
Bear the brunt, in a minute pay glad life's arrears
Of pain, darkness, and cold.
For sudden the worst turns the best to the brave,
The black mountain's at end,
And the elements rage, the fiend-voices that rave,
Shall dwindle, shall blend,
Shall change, shall become first a peace out of pain,
Then a light, then thy breast.
O thou soul of my soul! I shall clasp thee again,
And with God be the rest."

Interviewer: Browning wrote that shortly after his
wife's death, didn't he, Senator?

Ervin: Yes, he did.

Interviewer: And he lived a long time, had many
"fights," and never backed down a single time?

Ervin: That's correct.

Interviewer: Unfortunately, hardly anyone writes
heroic poetry today, or takes the hero for his subject. I
believe there is a saying among the people of the

136

Caucasian mountains that "Heroism is endurance for one moment more." But that, and everything Tennyson and Browning believed may be arrant heresy today, in many quarters.

Ervin: John Milton looked at it this way: "A man may be a heretic in the truth; and if he believes things only because his pastor says so, or the assembly so determines, without knowing other reasons, though his belief be true, yet the very truth he holds becomes his heresy."

Interviewer: Yes sir, and today if many of us approve an opinion we call it an "opinion," but those who don't approve it, call it "heresy."

Ervin: I remember this, from somewhere:

" 'Twixt the optimist and pessimist
The difference is droll:
The optimist sees the doughnut
But the pessimist sees the hole."

Interviewer: I believe it was Chauncey Depew, in one of his celebrated after-dinner speeches, who said, "A pessimist is a man who thinks all women are bad. An optimist is a man who hopes they are."

James Branch Cabell, the Virginia writer, put it this way: "The optimist proclaims that we live in the best of all possible worlds; and the pessimist fears this is true."

Ervin: Samuel Johnson believed that hope, itself, is a species of happiness, perhaps, the chief happiness.

Interviewer: Emily Dickinson put her hope to poetry:

"Hope is the thing with feathers
That perches in the soul,

And sings the tune without the words,
And never stops at all."

X

But, Senator, I see that clock on your desk is not diverted at all by Dr. Johnson, that it doesn't pause and turn aside to mull over Emily Dickinson's feathers in the soul. On a day such as this there is always the desire to bribe time, really to implore, as Ralph Hodgson beseeched, "Time, you old gypsy man,/Will you not stay,/Put up your caravan,/Just for a day?"

Ervin: Job said, "My day's are swifter than a weaver's shuttle."

Interviewer: Yes sir, and before our talk ends I'd like to ask you this: Who are the most unusual men our local society has produced?

Ervin: Now, by "unusual," do you mean men and women of tremendous merit, tremendous native endowments, or do you mean outrageous, men, men so bizarre their flaring personalities aren't likely to be duplicated?

Interviewer: The latter, Senator. North Carolina has produced, has at the moment, so many fine preachers, teachers, lawyers, scientists, doctors, business men, writers, thinkers, and doers it would be an impossible, unfair, task to ask you to pick out even a few of them for special comment.

Ervin: I doubt that any society had a more outrageous or bizarre personality than Robert Potter, of Granville County. Potter was a lawyer, a legislator, a Congressman, a classic example of the stormy petrel. His brief, tempestuous life was filled with so much violence, it is hard to separate fact from folklore.

He had a vendetta with members of a prominent Granville County family, and he castrated two, a clergyman and the clergyman's brother-in-law. Now, no law had been passed relative to this felonious act, and I understand Potter was tried and fined for assaulting the two men.

Interviewer: Several years after this happened, two Granville County ladies were talking and one of them mentioned the clergyman. Her friend said "Who?" and the lady replied, "You know, the gentleman whom Robert Potter treated so uncivilly."

Ervin: Yes, well the next general assembly passed a law making castration a felony. Potter was a member and he voted for the act, and for the next hundred years North Carolina judges and lawyers referred to this as the "Potter Act."

Potter was in jail, in Hillsborough, for safekeeping, I believe, and he was elected to Congress while he was in jail.

Interviewer: A cynic would say that's the reversal of natural order, that a Congressman should end up, not begin, in jail. But you know I am joshing.

Ervin: So was Mark Twain when he said: Let us assume that a man is an idiot and goes to Congress. But, I repeat myself."

Potter committed much of his political career to wild poetry, and much of this is available today. It's almost as if he kept a flamboyant, highly subjective diary in form of wooly narrative verse.

Finally, members of the family of the two men whom he castrated began pressing Potter pretty hard. One man, Colonel Taylor, had a shoot-out with Potter on Oxford's Main Street. Apparently, Potter was coming out of the courthouse, and the first time I ever held Superior Court in Oxford I was shown bullet holes in the enormous, heavy front door of the courthouse.

Interviewer: Was Potter hit?

Ervin: I don't think so, but he must have thought his sands were running out in North Carolina. He went to Texas and he became Secretary of the Navy under President Sam Houston, when Texas was a republic.

Interviewer: Texas's navy was about equal to the present navy of Switzerland? When did Potter die?

Ervin: Yes, about the size of the Swiss navy.

While the date of Potter's death is somewhat obscure, he was killed in a brawl somewhere on the Red River, in the eighteen forties.

Interviewer: There is the story, not supposed to be apocryphal, about the time Potter prosecuted a man named Finger, who was accused of shooting someone. Potter really poured it on Finger in his speech to the jury. Potter said the other man was seated in Oxford's Eagle Tavern, in quiet meditation, when Finger came in and shot him.

"There he was sitting, gentlemen of the jury, saying his meditations, when Mr. Pistol, like a thief in the night, came in waving his finger. Then Mr. Pistol came closer and placed his finger against the poor man's chest."

141

The other lawyers and several members of the jury howled at Potter's verbal confusion, at his having Mr. Pistol come waving his finger, and I understand Potter issued challenges to half the folks in the courthouse.

Ervin: Yes, I believe he was put in jail for contempt, and that the man who had been shot by "Mr. Pistol" went to jail with Potter, just for the temporary pleasure of his company.

Interviewer: That's my understanding. Now, Senator, how about a bizarre man of merit and character?

Ervin: Well, from several dozen really extraordinary "characters," I'd go with Judge Charles M. Cooke, whom we talked about earlier in the day.

Interviewer: The judge who told the court stenographer, "Hell, I don't know. You got one and I ain't?"

Ervin: The very same. I was in his court once when the judge was old and prone to doze off now and then. This somewhat pompous, opinionated lawyer was making a motion when he noticed that Judge Cooke had dozed off, his white head in the palm of his right hand. With a series of sneers the lawyer turned to his associates and the other court officials and exclaimed, "What can I do when the court is fast asleep?"

Judge Cooke rubbed his eyes and said, in an even voice: "Counsellor, you can go on with your motion, or you can go on to dinner, or you can go to hell. This court knows more law fast asleep under a haystack than counsel knows with all the answers to all the questions given on the bar examination for fifty years."

As a boy, Judge Cooke had fought in the Confederate army, and he was always zealous for the welfare of his old comrades. Three trials illustrate his attitude. This

Confederate veteran, about seventy-five, went around the countryside selling herbs and roots. The father of a young girl had the Confederate veteran indicted for fornication and adultery. Now, the herbs and roots were cracked-up to be potent, and the old fellow said he ate them everyday.

About the time the young girl finished testifying to the fact of fornication with the old man, Judge Cooke boomed out: "Enough of this. I hope God strikes me dead if I ever find a Confederate veteran guilty of anything. Old man, you are free to go. Get on out of here."

As the old man, his gunny sack of herbs and roots on his shoulder, neared the door leading from the courthouse, Judge Cooke hollered out: "Old man, the court wants a private consultation with you, in chambers, upon adjournment this afternoon, and I mean with your sack of herbs and roots with you."

Another aged Confederate veteran was indicted for bastardy, and again the woman was a young girl. The old soldier entered a plea of guilty. Judge Cooke broke in: "Old man, haven't I seen you somewhere before?"

"You might have, Judge, if you ever saw the old Sixth North Carolina Infantry Regiment in action. I fought in that regiment for four years."

"And a better outfit never wore shoe leather, when it could find shoes. Mr. Clerk, strike this old man's plea of guilty. This old fool's just bragging."

A third former Confederate was arrested for violating the new North Carolina prohibition laws. He and two non-veterans had been standing beside a hedge and in the hedge was a quantity of white whiskey. The other two men ran, or left, and the old soldier remained. The solicitor contended that the old fellow's staying by the hedge was prima facie evidence of possession, of ownership.

But Judge Cooke looked down from the bench at his former comrade-in-arms, then looked over at the solicitor and said: "The hell with that line of argument. 'The wicked flee when no man approaches.' Case dismissed."

Interviewer: Well, Senator, that clock on your desk tells me we have reached the end of what has been a most delightful journey for me. As Tar Heels used to say, "The old Ark's a-mouverin'," and I better get on board. But tomorrow I will know that tremendous sense of loss that enveloped Douglas Southall Freeman when he finished his four-volumed biography of Robert E. Lee.

Mrs. Freeman told her husband that he seemed ill at ease, and he replied: "Yes, I am, but you see, my dear, I have been intimately in the company of a very great man for a long time and right now I am extremely lonely."

It would be fulsome for me to quote the old lady who said, "No, I have never seen God but I talked with General Lee." But I do thank you, Senator, from the bottom of my heart for this memorable experience. Although I came too late to sit at the feet of Gamaliel, I can tell my grandchildren how, on a happy, proud day, I rubbed elbows and stories with Senator Sam Ervin. I'll remind my grandchildren of the old saying, "A good man is as tall as his own height, plus his learning, and the length of his own home-town." And I'll tell them that Senator Sam Ervin measured out, from his soles to his crown, ten miles of wise goodness, plus five-feet-ten.

***

MOORE books about national figures and events are:

Ralph McGill At Work, Vol. I   Calvin Logue, Ph.D.
Ralph McGill Speaks, Vol. II
    These major books about Ralph McGill and his works are written by a professor at the University of Georgia who knew and interviewed Ralph McGill, who was the courageous voice of the South at a time in the civil rights movement when courage was at a premium.

The Life and Accomplishments of Herbert Hoover
                                   Walter L. Miller
    The author was in the administration of Mr. Hoover and puts into perspective the greatness of a man remembered for the economic crisis of the great depression and who tried so desperately to restore confidence in our nation.

The Gentleman From Ohio   Richard O. Bates
(An Introduction To Garfield)
    The author is a retired midwestern newspaper man who has always had a thing about the President who deserves more attention than he has received.

Sarah and Abe In Indiana   Adin Baber
    The author is a descendant of Nancy Hanks Lincoln and presents a side of Abraham Lincoln and his sister, and of their childhood, that has never been presented with such warm understanding.

Metric 16   Meredith L. Butterton

This is the story of an ordinance company assigned to the 9th Infantry Division and contributed to Generals Eisenhower, Bradley, Collins, Ridgway, Gavin, Taylor and others, each registering his own personal and now historical candid expression.

The Ballad of Tom Dula   John Foster West

In this book, John Foster West analyzes a legend as thoroughly as one can from a century away. Although time erodes memory, certain truths come out of his many efforts and they are carefully reconstructed.

Rx For America   Eugene V. Grace, M. D.

A discussion of various health options by an author concerned with delivery and financing of health care.

Dangers To Children and Youth   Jay Arena, M. D.

A guide for families in which the care of young people is important, written by the immediate past president of the American Academy of Pediatrics.

Rhetoric of Revolution   Andrea Rich and Arthur Smith

These professors of communication compare the rhetoric of Samuel Adams, Emma Goldman and Malcolm X and define their roles in influencing the opinions of Americans.

DATE DUE

DE 6 77			
OC 27 83			
REC 3 '86			
GAYLORD			PRINTED IN U.S A.